Trappings of a big company

Trappings of a big company

Jaideep Sen

ISBN-13: 9781533376718
ISBN-10: 1533376719
Library of Congress Control Number: 2016908685
CreateSpace Independent Publishing Platform
North Charleston, South Carolina

Contents

Acknowledgments

This book is a compilation of several years of learning and experience working in different companies and living in different countries. I am thankful to have interacted with so many wonderful people during the journey. I apologize that I will not be able to call out everybody's name here, but know that you contributed to this book.

My wife, Neeta, for being a creative genius and supporting me through all the waves of our life and to my son, Anshuman, for always inspiring me to take on newer challenges.

The innumerable friends and colleagues from the last forty years, from whose experiences I have drawn strength and insights.

My parents Malaya and Kalpana, who have always been there for me, every step of the way.

My uncle Syamal Gupta, who has always been an inspiration and who has shown exception leadership qualities that I have always learned from, and my uncle Moloy Gupta, whose grit, resilience, and perseverance are unmatchable. The entire Gupta family for being such an inspiration to the world, especially Kajal Gupta and Bimal Gupta. My uncle Dipak Sen for being there for me during my engineering days.

All my cousins for showing a lot of faith in what I do and always standing by me.

Professor Mike Tushman at Harvard Business School for those words of wisdom, "Up your game."

My cohort at Harvard Business School: Adrian Stewart, Amer Jarragh, Hena Rana, Melanie Humphries, Patrick Tomlinson, Mark Brooks, and Jason Greene. The entire PLD18 class, which made the Harvard Business School experience unforgettable. The PLD faculty, including professors Amy Cuddy, Gary Pisano, Eugene Soltes, Lakshmi Iyer, Eric Van den Steen, and John Gourville.

All the wonderful people who have worked on my team in the last several years.

All the leaders, mentors, and friends I have worked with and learned from, including Ravi Venkatesan, Pallavi Kathuria, Keith White, Doug Hauger, Turi Widsteen, Tarun Gulati, Neelam Dhawan, Chandy Bilugu, Sashi Kumar, Chris Capossela, Steve Brown, Rajan Anandan, Zane Adam, Michel Gambier, James Hutchinson, Ed Anderson, Sudev Muthya, Shrikant Patil, Garth Fort, Kalyan Kumar, Stephanie Ferguson, Takeshi Numoto, Sashi Kumar, Chris Sharp, Gavriella Schuster, Tami Yamashita, Brian Hillger, Karan Bajwa, Srikanth Karnakota, Radhesh Balakrishnan, Vinesh Paperwala, Raj Gill, Vinish Kathuria, Ashish Khare, Erica Lill, Roxy Stimpson, Michael Heijer, Jayant Swamy, Maurice Martin, Michel N'Guettia, Anne-Lise Touati, Harp Girn, Maria Ilieva, Arun Ulag, Selma Karaca, Bill O'Brien, Karan Khanna, Krishan Chander Vijay, Saroj Vijay, Sushant Banerjee, Gunjan Banerjee, Sunil C, Anita S, Ajit Moodliar, Sudha Moodliar, Hema Muthya, Giri Bhaskara, Deepa V, Rajan Bisht, Vandana, Fazal Khan, Dia Khan, Sandy Sharma, Prasenjit Dasgupta, Nandita Sharma, Lena Powers, Shira Fayans – Birenbaum, James G Wilders Reed, Gitesh Vijay, Nilakshi Bansal, Ravi Bansal, Srikanth Matcha, Praveen Khanna, Anurag Pahwa, Vidhi Anand, Shilpa

Khanna, Devyani Matcha, Joseph O'Neill, Sameer Chaudhri, Sakshi Chaudhri, Karun Thareja, Rohit Sarkar, Rajiv Sodhi, Amit Kumar, Alok Lall, and several others who have been an inspiration in this journey.

This is my first book, so I am sure these pages contain a few errors, which are totally unintentional. For those, I ask for your forgiveness and take full responsibility.

Foreword

I have spent over sixteen years of my career working in large companies in different places across the world. I have learned a lot from my own experiences and from those of my friends and colleagues. This book is a compilation of my experiences and those of other hardworking people who make big companies successful and who spend their lives building their careers in big companies.

If I had hung in there for another ten years, I would have retired comfortably. One fine day early 2016, I decided to pull the plug, disrupt myself, and stop what I was doing to go live my dreams. This is not the first time I have disrupted myself, but probably the first time I made such a bold decision. With no paycheck coming in and a family to support, it is a hard call to leave an awesome job in a great company.

A lot of people reached out to me after I quit and the number-one thing they told me was that they would love to do the same thing and start living their dreams. Not everybody wants to quit their jobs, but they want to do more and be in the right place that inspires them to get to work every day.

I have been writing this book bit by bit over these years capturing my experiences against the backdrop of the global technological and ideological revolution taking place. These experiences from having worked in big companies are interesting learnings that I wanted to share with all of you.

As per the Oxford dictionary, 'Trappings' refer to "the outward signs, features, or objects associated with a particular situation, role or job". This book is about the features and signs associated with big companies.

STOP

Stop doing things you dislike. I come across so many people who complain about stress at work. People tell me that they want to live their dreams but are trapped in their own reasons for not being able to do so. Stress is a function of the goals we set and the aspirations we have and in most cases, self-created. I realized that the number-one thing that forces us to do jobs we do not like is security. What will happen to my house if I quit? What about shopping? Kids' education? Lifestyle? Cars?

However, once you quit or break free, you'll find that these are the least of your problems. First you lose the primary stress-creating factors, which were really material in nature—all the things we need to have and possess. Once you overcome that, you realize that you're automatically happier. If you are reasonably smart, hardworking, and educated, you will always earn enough to do things that you want and to live happy. Nine out of ten people told me that I looked happier after I quit my job. It wasn't because I had a bad deal at my previous company—it was because I was living my dreams. So stop doing what you dislike.

SENSE

Sense what you want to do. This is important in order to succeed in business. What do you do when you're ready to disrupt yourself and take a new course in life? It would be foolish to quit one day and leave things to fate, or randomly change to a new role just to get a feel for what it's like to do something different. Sense what you want to do before you make such a decision. Sensing will give you a glimpse of the future that can make you happy.

People who can sense opportunities (and problems) quicker are usually more adept at driving clarity of vision and execution. Be in control of what you do while living your dreams. Do a reality check on your dreams and be self-aware of what you are capable of.

START

Start doing what you like best. At some point, you have to start living your dreams. The worst that can happen is that you won't make it. That's the same state you'd be in if you didn't try.

When you start something, activate all the muscles in your ecosystem. Go the full way. Engage and invest in people inside (employees) or outside (customers) the organization. Start today as if there is no tomorrow.

Business is all about relationships, and it takes place in the cultural backdrop of the socio-economic system you live in. The

US housing crisis, the Greek financial crisis, oil-price changes, Chinese currency issues, US presidential elections—all of them have a deep impact on your business, wherever you are. Leaders are like the captains of ships negotiating one big wave after another, docking at a port for a few days, and moving on again. It is a journey with short milestones in between. We need to enjoy not only the milestones but each moment of the journey.

A lot of people live for the milestones and give their sweat and blood to reach the next one, and, when they reach it, they find yet another milestone to achieve. At some point, the journey becomes endless and looks helpless. The people who are energized and have fun during the journey are happy.

There are others who are stressed and live their lives like robots going from one milestone to another. If you feel like the later, you need to stop and think. There are leadership and organizational attributes and your own self that cause stress and send clear signals for you to stop (in your tracks) and change direction. That might mean quitting your job, taking a different role in the same company, or creating a development plan for yourself. To be able to do this, you also need to pick the right opportunities, be ahead of the curve, and feel good about the journey you are on. If you don't, take a different path or embark on a different journey.

Business is really a people game. Whether you're selling technology solutions, building products, or running an airline, your people will be the ultimate determinants of your success in the marketplace. Setting the right culture to keep people engaged and activated will be the key to success.

One

SCrew It to Fix It (SCIFI)

*Opportunity is missed by most people because
it is dressed in overalls and looks like work.*

—Thomas Alva Edison

I am driving to work on a rainy Seattle morning in October. It
is a Wednesday, and I'm happy that it's close to the weekend
(Wednesday is kind of close) I'm listening to my favorite Bender
and Molly morning show on Kiss FM, but my mind is somewhere else—at work. Earlier in the week, something happened,
and I thought we were missing a big opportunity. For several
years, this question has been nagging me—why do big companies miss opportunities?

After working for several years at large multinational companies, I think I finally found an answer to this question during this drive. It has to do with the culture and leadership style that is practiced in big companies. It is not as if there is a dearth of ideas or a lack of smart people. Large companies have highly qualified and experienced people, and those same people are usually successful when they work in startups or newer ventures. Why do opportunities not show up the same way in a large company? The issue is really one of philosophy and how big corporations are set up to handle opportunities.

A new senior vice president at a large oil and gas company presented to the leadership team ways to reduce gasoline loss and leakage through distribution channels in third-world countries. He covered in great detail all measures that would be required to address this issue, such as better delivery and distribution systems, new weight-based measurement systems, and intelligent tracking. He went on to talk about the long-term return on investment and some creative ideas that the company should consider, including implementing sensor-based technologies on delivery tankers. At the end of the presentation, he was told that the presentation was screwed up because he was paid to "do stuff and fix things" and not waste time in creative strategy. This may be an extreme example.

Despite having highly capable people who can think ahead of the curve and unearth early opportunity, the system usually pushes them back. Time and again, I sat through leadership meetings and reviews where we spent hours belaboring business as usual and missed out on the big things that would drive transformation. Many people participate in important meetings to checkmark that they were present and, even if they contributed nothing meaningful to the discussions. Sometimes they quote from the meetings to show their importance and throw names around. That's where it stops, and the system does not allow ideas to germinate.

A new idea is a hard sell—harder to sell internally than to sell externally to customers. Organizations need to find ways to be more open to new ideas and to empower people to take risks. We need to hire and retain people who can continuously think beyond their jobs to drive aspirational advantage in their businesses, irrespective of their hierarchical level in the company. In many cultures, hierarchy acts as a bar to creativity.

We need to keep those people motivated and engaged. Organizations that can't nurture new ideas usually end up losing good talent. The people who are hard to retain are those who think they can make a difference to their careers and to the world by trying out something different.

In my twenty-two years of working across different countries, I have come across numerous leaders who promote a culture of "status quo," which equates to let ideas go by.

My first theory is that they wait for ideas to mature or ripen—ideas are not ideas unless they have critical mass, and many senior executives in big companies believe in waiting it out till they hear more people talking about the same ideas. I often chat with business leaders about potential opportunities, and, almost every time, these *wait-and-watch* (WAW) leaders come back with the same answer: "Wait for it to mature. This is not the right time to do this."

In the technology-enabled world of today, this is an unhealthy approach for organizations. Speed is of the essence. In almost every industry, technology can leapfrog a business model multiple times, and you cannot wait and watch. Every new idea is a potential startup, with some of them having the potential to destroy your business. WAW behavior sometimes becomes a cultural trait, which means people start believing in it like it is corporate gospel, and the organization unknowingly patronizes a "wait-and-watch" culture.

As I look back at some of the "wait-and-watch" leaders, I find that the whole team eventually starts thinking the same way. In fact, the downstream teams do so much waiting and watching that they don't do anything at all. Such leaders in big companies get attuned to addressing only mature ideas and resolving bigger problems.

My second theory is that some leaders feel that new ideas challenge an existing paradigm, which, in their minds, equates to failure of existence. How can there be something new when they have been doing their jobs so well and are getting paid for it? To protect themselves and their jobs, they try to force fit to existing plans. New ideas are threats to the current leaders or team because they believe they are rock stars and have every-thing figured out. While this is true at times, -this behavior usu-ally becomes a bottleneck to unearthing new opportunities.

I have experimented with this several times (and you can try this out, just for fun) by sharing ideas with people to test their reactions. Most of the time, this resulted in a mad scramble to prove why the new ideas were already covered within the existing plans. The more credible you are, the harder they have to try.

And it doesn't stop there. Sometimes, people silently copy those ideas into their plans, which is good for the company but fails to create a muscle for sensing ideas and opportunities and is ultimately a cultural disaster. This is what I call as *Protect your ASS (PASS)* leadership. The most important thing on their minds is protecting their jobs, the work they do, and the franchises they built. The output is secondary.

One of my friends from Harvard works at a consulting company that has been trying for years to operationalize new process changes for its engineering projects. The company's projects slowed down, and failures increased. He tried so hard to bring in the new process changes that he became a pain in their necks. He was removed from his job and given a side project. In the meantime, other folks secretly started implementing his ideas, but they got stuck halfway through. The leadership got wind of this, and they brought him back. He was eventually made head of the team that was working on the changes and the new processes, but they lost precious time.

Most people do not have the tenacity or energy to fight back, but if you do, it usually pays off. These leaders are usually nice and accommodating, but they are reactive in their approach. They miss opportunities and ideas when they are most relevant and always start late. They usually jump on the bandwagon when a senior leader or the boss tells them that the idea is great. This "after-the-fact" and reactive leadership style does not help create competitive advantage for companies, and they start falling behind competitors.

Finally, and this is the best of the lot for me—the category of leaders that lets opportunities go by and waits for business to screw up so that it becomes a disaster. Once something is on the verge of disaster, they step in to help solve the big problem or work on the big opportunity. They are like "firefighters" with the personal goal of becoming heroes to gets them faster career growth. Unfortunately, by the time the ideas are addressed or fixed, precious time has passed, and results in a serious loss of competitive advantage that is not even realized till later. I call this *SCIFI—SCrew It to Fix It.*

So how do you run or be part of organizations and get past WAW, PASS, or SCIFI leaders? How do you distinguish good ideas from the not-so-good ones that take up a lot of time? Practice and encourage the art of sensing.

Sensing is the ability to identify and activate an opportunity at the right time. Imagine a situation where hundreds of people in your organization sense opportunities at the right time and aligned to a common set of goals. This will unleash a potent competitive advantage that is unparalleled and unachievable through any training or readiness.

Sensing is not just about new opportunities at work. It can come in useful in day-to-day life and can make life interesting. We gauge and sense people and situations when we interact with them. For example, you know more about a person when you meet in person for the first time than when you connect virtually. This is information you can use—like when somebody repeats a sentence or when pauses more than necessary. Or when it seems that somebody has reached a foregone conclusion or is totally disconnected and staring at the computer, clearly not interested in what you are saying.

This is the same way you can sense opportunities. There are various aspects of sensing that can help companies identify opportunities faster and solve problems quicker. Ultimately, this will also help reduce stress and make you happier, because you are somewhat prepared in what is coming your way.

Great leaders are "sensetionaries"—they can sense, create a vision, and engage the whole organization to work toward that vision. They are not shy about taking risks and experimenting with bold new ideas or letting their employees do so. I have worked with some of these leaders (many of them at Microsoft), and it is highly energetic, stress-reducing, and exciting to work with them. Every time you work with a "sensetionary," you feel inspired, motivated, and eager to put in your best effort. They usually have uniform acceptance and likeability. Once they set the vision, they let others take ownership and do things their way. Not every employee in an organization will end up becoming the CEO, but, by practicing sensing and risk-taking, you can make a big difference for yourself and for the organization. You can set a culture that will promote creativity, ideation, and higher value creation for the company.

Two

Old-Boys' Club

*I am not afraid of an army of lions led by a
sheep; I am afraid of an army of sheep led by
a lion.*

—ALEXANDER THE GREAT

A few days after the Wednesday morning drive, I got a call from one of my friends in Singapore. He worked in a financial-services firm and found it difficult to navigate the organization and get approval on strategic initiatives. He is new at this job. Despite being a solid networker and people's person, he was getting stuck. In addition, the hunt for resources and information was driving him insane. I gave him a few ideas and hung up. It reminded me of the tech company I worked for several years back where I hit roadblocks in the first few months.

There is an old-boys' club everywhere, and a lot has been written about it. However, these clubs are not just about a group of men trying to keep women out. That might be where some of them started, but they're broader now. If you take a global view of things, you'll see that these clubs can impact different kinds of employees; for example, new hires, outspoken people, less-confident people, alumni, and so on. The degree to which this happens varies from country to country and culture to culture.

In many big companies, the old-boys' club makes key decisions—it is definitely the power center and the nerve center of the organization. Big companies usually have more than one boys' club—these people negotiate with each other, play with each other, and sometimes fight with each other. The good news is that if you can reach the club and gain its attention, you can get anything done. If you find your way to the nerve center, you'll know exactly what nerve to press to get a desired outcome. The flip side is that the club decides everything—you are not the real decision-maker on things of strategic importance.

These clubs can sometimes have a positive impact on an organization—they can help new people onboard faster, solve problems and interpersonal issues, and remove bottlenecks. But if they aren't progressive enough, they can deter organizational growth and culture.

Back to my example of the tech company from several years back. I not only hit roadblocks but was stonewalled by groups of people as I worked on critical initiatives. At one point, I thought about giving up because I wasn't able to make any headway. But I leaned in and played it out; I kept working at it.

One day there was a customer event, and our keynote speaker dropped out at the last minute because he was sick. I seemed to be the only person who could deliver that talk, and the boys' club nominated me. In a few hours, I was talking to a whole bunch of customers on a favorite topic of mine. The feedback was positive, and a lot of customers wanted to have a follow-up conversation with me. That changed everything. From being an outsider to the clubs, I became the most sought after guy in town. I not only got into the clubs, but also started hanging out with folks outside work. This was a situation where the impact of the clubs was positive, and so it helped.

Historically, these clubs have been male-dominated. Even now, most people on these clubs are men. They hang out together, drink beer and coffee, and make strategic decisions together. And they are not old by any means—it's just that they worked long enough in the organization to be called old.

The clubs, however, have become more diverse, and, in many cases, they work on a broader charter. I know one club in an organization that was run by a woman—I thought that was a great way to break the male-dominant clubs.

When you take on a new job or a new role, especially one where the team members have been around long enough, you may face an old-boys' club. Sometimes you'll have to force your way in; other times you'll just have to let them be. Sometimes you'll have to force people out if you have authority over their work. The one thing you have to figure out quickly is whether the clubs are good for the business and create value. If they are, figure out ways to align with them, influence them, and lead them. If the clubs are mostly change-resistant and disruptive, expose them and get rid of them as quickly as possible.

When these clubs are change-resistant, you'll find it harder to push through new ideas. This will be harder than selling to customers, because some of the change might be deemed to challenge the mere existence of these clubs. People in change-resistant clubs prefer the status quo and you will find a lot of WAWs and PASSs in these clubs. This is a pseudo-unionized way of holding things together. The only time they budge is when they see real value creation or when their customers tell them that something needs to change. Many times, this happens late in the game and competitive advantage is lost. As a leader, you'll have to quickly organize your act and establish a position.

A friend of mine, Susan, ran a business division in a financial-services company. For several months, she felt like an outsider. While everybody was supportive, she felt that there was more getting discussed than she was privy to. In many cases, discussions about new projects came up in meetings, catching her by surprise, while some of her peers seemed to know about it.

She decided to talk to her boss, the CEO, and he seemed to know nothing about it. Eventually she discovered that some of these people played golf together, and their families hung out together during weekends. There was nothing wrong with it, except that they discussed business, and the others, like her, didn't know about it.

How do you go about addressing such a situation? Do you start playing golf with them and start hanging out on the weekends? For one, socializing definitely helps. It helps break the ice and lets people see hidden perspectives. These informal alignments often don't happen for any evil reason but out of sheer fraternity and the feeling of belongingness. Business is all about people, so whether you like it or not, you have to network aggressively, because business happens only through people. But sometimes, when socializing gets to a point that you do not like, you can say no.

Susan decided that she couldn't possibly network with these people outside of work because her interests were different. Instead, she decided to talk to them and make them understand that their approach was creating a problem for her and others.

She always had to catch up. It took her a lot of time, but she eventually got them to see her point of view.

These clubs also act as the supreme court of the company—they pass judgments. In many cases, they pass these judgments in the presence of a broad set of other employees so that they understand the "law" of the company. They act as custodians of the unwritten rules in the company and make sure this is visible and apparent. Sometimes these are beneficial to the organization at large but may not always help solve larger problems.

The famous saying in big companies (I don't know where it came from) is that a tested "strategy is to throw a lot of shit at the wall and hope that some of it will stick." Or at the least will leave a mark behind that will let people know they tried. What this means is that when you are unsure of your strategy, experiment with a few ideas and hope that one of them works. This strategy is based on hope and is usually used when people have less knowledge of their markets, customers, or ecosystems. These ideas often come from the boys' club because they are focused inward.

When you have large organizations, with hundreds of people and different teams and several clubs, there are a lot of such ideas flying around. It often becomes unmanageable, real opportunities get lost, and it is a waste of time. If you are a newbie, you can see and smell this from a distance. If you are an existing person who has lived and grown with that environment, you will likely not see it anymore. As a business leader, it is important to dig in and question generic approaches to business. For example, recycled strategy plans immediately raise a flag for me. Generic investment proposals, training plans, all raise flags here. I have looked through a lot of business plans with nice ideas, but, when I dug deeper, I found that most of them were not practically implementable.

There is a chance that we could get involved with or become dependent on one or more of these clubs and not realize the consequences. Therefore, it is always good to step back and take stock of things. Are you open enough to new ideas? Are you fully aware of what is happening in the market to be able to make meaningful decisions? Are you supporting global diversity?

My friend James told me about this bank where he had worked long enough to become part of the boys' club. One day, when he was talking to a new hire, he realized he was being negative to every new idea and found a justification for why something wouldn't work whenever somebody came up with an idea. He realized that he must have turned down numerous people and not listened to the ideas and concepts they pitched to him. He would have potentially lost several opportunities since he was not open enough and was trying to protect his franchise.

We must avoid falling into this trap. One way is to question and challenge the status quo. In many large organizations, the "real authority" to challenge and question usually lies with the highest ranked person in the meeting or in the room. Assuming that this person knows the most and asks the right questions is nonsensical. This is hierarchal leadership and where things start going wrong. Sometimes the boys' clubs are associated with strong hierarchal positions so they play a key role in pushing back on new ideas and opportunities. We must all push ourselves to explore new ideas and challenge the status quo.

These clubs also have shifting philosophies, and they shift left or right to move from one pressure point to another. Take an example of a technology company. If the company has a strong sales force, it is able to comprehend and translate customer requirements into how they can be fulfilled. They put pressure on engineering and marketing folks to create the right products and services and get them to market quicker. The pressure moves from sales to engineering.

If you have an organization where the engineering team is stronger, it tends to push and dominate most of the product roadmap and strategy, and that gets pushed to sales. That pressure requires them to pitch harder to customers. Most organizations go through such multiple shifts in their lifecycle.

When you have a strong product or service company, the pressure moves to the sales team, and it needs to figure out ways to manage that pressure to meet customer demand. In an ideal situation, the clubs need to comprehend and manage such shifts. I have seen numerous examples where the pressure has been so intense that the organization gets completely dysfunctional, with people doing overlapping tasks. I have seen situations where product engineers spend more time in sales situations and less time in building the products. Or sales people who spend way too much time troubleshooting product-engineering problems. The overall entropy of the system remains the same, and it is the job of the leadership to make sure that they don't shift way too much to one side. The clubs need to act as buffers to shifting business units and hold them together. In times of change, these clubs can work as connective tissue across the organization to hold the business units together.

Building and growing an organization is an art and needs a lot of creativity. You need creative business artists who are original thinkers and can sense the right opportunities to pursue. I have seen the same strategy get deployed year after year in newer PowerPoint templates. There are times when process requirements trump business needs. I have seen use of brute vocal force and body language by leaders to keep the status quo. This erodes long-term value and employee confidence in an organization. The clubs can play moderating roles, especially when working with dysfunctional leaders. It doesn't happen all the time, especially since the clubs follow their own agendas and they don't always align 100 percent with the organization's goals.

Like I said before, having informal associations aka the boys' club among leaders is not always a bad sign. Sometimes they drive positive energy and actually make things move faster. They also need to be dynamic enough to be open to new ideas, be inclusive, diverse, and be cognizant of and aligned with the overall company goals and culture. They also drive silos within organizations that prevent cross-group collaboration between people.

Credit goes to Satya Nadella and his effort in turning around Microsoft. A company full of talented people and steeped in pockets of brilliance—he dove right in to break the silos and get people, groups, and teams to work together more than ever before. Cultural change in such a big company takes time and needs everybody to lean in, but they have a great start with the leader setting the theme for cultural change in the company. I cannot forget the moment in 2014, when I was seated in the front row of a classroom at Harvard. Professor Mike Tushman walked up to me and asked if I had read the newspaper that morning. I (shamefully) said no and he pointed out an interview with Nadella on culture change at Microsoft. We spent a good amount of time talking about the impact of culture change and why it is important for organizations to survive in the long run and I felt proud to represent Microsoft in that discussion.

A few days after the discussion with my friend from Singapore, I called him to find out how things were going. He was happy because he had made good progress after he accidentally connected with somebody (part of the steering committee for this project) whose children went to the same school as his children. He explained his situation, and the guy promised to help him out, which he did.

A former colleague of mine was always on the lookout for such opportunities. There were times when he would dial senior leaders, tell them he had called by mistake, and end up chatting with them—like a cold call. This is an extreme example, but you need to be a savvy networker to be part of the club quickly. There is no point in shying away from the clubs or taking them head on—unless you have solid sponsorship. The best thing to do is to work with them and make them better. Join the right power centers and not just the hobbyists. Once you're inside, it's easier to influence them and change them so that they are more open to new ideas and change. You can then turn these clubs into veritable, long-term assets for the company.

Three

Chief Orchestration Officer

All these things need to be coordinated; so we all need to work together, have timers going and everything so we're all coordinated and get this piece of orchestration done.

—Duane G Carey

Christmas is just around the corner, and people are wrapping things up for the holidays. In several parts of the world, this is a time when people wind down for the holidays to spend time with friends and family. For me, it is also a good time to reflect on the year gone by.

I was talking to a tech-industry recruiter from the Bay Area during the week before Christmas. He was hiring for leadership positions for a small company that was projected to grow big, and they needed people who could scale and grow that organization. I thought those were great skills to be found in people working in big organizations. He disagreed and told me that he is wary of finding the right talent within big companies because it is hard to find people who roll up their sleeves and do the actual work themselves. According to him, they are good at orchestrating and coordinating work, but the actual works gets done elsewhere.

While this hypothesis is true in pockets, I thought it was an exaggeration. Being bigger means you have more layers to manage and more complexity all around. It takes time to peel the layers to get to the real stuff, but leaders have figured out ways to do it. There are people who stay hidden within these layers, and it's hard to separate the good talent from the not-so-good. But I never realized that the perception was as negative as he was projecting it to be. This recruiter eventually hired his people from other midsize companies, and they are doing well today, but the thought persisted in my head, and I decided to dig deeper.

Orchestration is an important part of any business with people and processes. Orchestration is required to create harmony in a business environment. Orchestration by itself and on a wrong strategy can be counterproductive and cannot trump business needs. I frequently come across people who play the role of "orchestrators." I call them chief orchestration officers. Their job is to simply orchestrate complex stuff, and, most of the time, they create even more complexity in the system. Usually, these chief orchestrating officers do not create anything of value or own any business tasks that create value. They are good process people with little knowledge of business or customers.

I have come across several orchestration officers at various levels within organizations who have less ability or intent to sense opportunities. Their ability to sense is low because their exposure to customers and business is low. Their primary job is to orchestrate and align resources in big companies. It doesn't usually work because adaptation and course correction is needed along the way, and these people usually don't have the business knowledge or customer centricity to make those changes or make those decisions. They become obsessed with the process, and, eventually, orchestration trumps business needs. This is one reason many big companies have slow innovation and growth—too much orchestration drags them back every time.

Companies have people working on multiple projects and diverse work streams. There is frequent need to coordinate, assimilate, or manage resources across priorities. Orchestration is everybody's responsibility. It's like a relay race where the baton needs to be passed from one athlete to the other. Even with higher levels of complexity, you don't need specialist orchestrators.

Sometimes these orchestrators are powerful, and they are huge survival geeks who know how to maneuver through organizations. I have seen organizations inadvertently penalize people for doing real work and reward people for being great orchestrators instead. If you are one of the people who actually do the work and create value for an organization, you'll likely be questioned and will find yourself defending the work you do.

These chief orchestration officers are good at questioning and probing—and are mostly seen at executive reviews. It can become frustrating because many of these people are not really equipped with adequate business knowledge to run a business—so the discussion is mostly meaningless. The difference between a business leader and an orchestrator is that the former knows the business and orchestrates as part of that, while the later just orchestrates and coordinates. Orchestrators are good at setting up meetings and reviews, doing a lot of landing exercises, and setting processes to manage things. These are all required to manage a complex business but cannot become the primary drivers and motivation for the business.

Orchestration also offers a broad framework for underperformers to stay hidden—because there is so much complexity in today's business environment that you can keep moving things, and nobody will notice. An orchestrator can continually move things around to create more complexity and work. A lot of people steer away from complexity, so pure-play orchestrators get a free hand. Eventually, the needle doesn't move on the business—but you get into massive business-as-usual discussions.

Orchestrators also find sponsorship in senior leaders, and this is one way for leaders to establish authority. If you want to be successful in the new corporate world, you need to know how to transform these roles into ones that create value for an organization.

One way to do this is to recalibrate these roles and retrain people to understand the business. Everybody needs to know their business, their market, and their customers. It will help them be relevant and do their jobs better. Orchestration without business alignment is meaningless. Rotate people into different roles, and orchestration should be a part of everybody's job rather than having a few people specialize in that function. I have come across several specialist orchestrators in the various organizations I have worked in. Sometimes it has been really hard to reason with them and get them to see business logic because they have been too focused on the orchestration process. In most of these situations, we ended up doing work-arounds which were short term fixes to the problem.

A friend of mine used to work in the loans department of a bank that was overtly run by processes and orchestration. They had extra people in the chain to validate every single application over and above what their compliance process required. This led to a bad experience for customers and the bank's business slowed down. The company started losing their best customer-facing people, while the process-control orchestrators became more powerful. Eventually, they realized that their share of bad loans was way higher than the industry standard. When my friend dug deeper, he found that the bank had lost genuine customers because of the additional time and complexity. The bank ended up with a lot of below-standard loans because the people who applied figured out how to beat the system through a standard process-led approach, and the orchestrators didn't have enough business knowledge to dig deeper into the merit of each case. Hence, they ended up with a lot of bad loans.

Going back to my discussion with the recruiter, I am still not convinced of his logic. I have seen big companies reorganize to cut a lot of flab. They are also trying to be more agile (more on agility later) by empowering people to do more. You need big-company experience to be able to scale businesses globally, and he agreed with this. He told me that there are still way too many hands-off orchestrators in big companies, and it is difficult to identify those as external recruiters, and I agreed with that.

Four

Self-Disruption

The key is to embrace disruption and change

early. Don't react to it decades later. You can't

fight innovation.

—RYAN KAVANAUGH

Disruption is a great topic for discussion when chatting with friends or when you read about it in a book. It is really hard to self-disrupt in real life. In early 2016 after several months of introspection, I left my coveted job in the cloud business at Microsoft to pursue my dreams. Some people called it hara-kiri, and some thought I was out of my mind. Why would one leave a job in a high-growth cloud business in one of the largest and most successful technology companies of the world? I had a great team and a great manager, and it was a great place to work. So why did I do it? This was self-disruption in the pursuit of my dreams.

I looked back at the twenty-two years of my working career and realized that I have done this a couple of times in the past, but never to this extent. After graduating as an engineer, I quickly switched to becoming a business leader because I was passionate about sales, marketing, and business development. I left my job at Hewlett-Packard to start a brand new and untested consulting services gig at Intel. Everybody who used to sit around me was laid off in a reorganization. I was scared, but I dug in and had one of the most wonderful professional experiences of my career.

I was settled in Asia when I moved to the United States several years back to start a new journey, a new life experience. Each of these disruptive decisions was highly enriching and took me to greater heights, but each time there was the fear of dealing with the unknown and the uncertainty associated with those decisions.

Why do I keep doing this again and again?

I don't like status quo and get bored quickly—I find it difficult to keep doing the same thing over and over again. I have seen a lot of WAW and PASS leaders who have let big opportunities go by. I love change—I love change squared, and I love driving change. While people used to worry about re-orgs, I watched for them and, if possible, influenced them. In the several years I worked in large companies, I had the opportunity to drive change, take on new challenges, and create new stuff. But I really needed to hunt for and nurture those opportunities—they didn't come easy and naturally. And I had to navigate the boys' clubs. I cherish the opportunity to create and build something new—this is a big one for me, I feel suffocated when I'm not able to create and build new stuff. I don't feel good being an orchestrator or being surrounded by several of them.

There are a few things that were different this time though. I quit but didn't have another job to go back to (I didn't want to). Every time, I quit on a Friday and went to work on Monday morning. This time, I had some ideas including the one about finishing this book, but I did not have any other venture or side gig going. This time, I quit to figure out what I really wanted to do. I wanted to build something new and path-breaking. And I didn't want to go back to another job on Monday morning, quite yet. Instead, I took a break for a few days, spent time with friends and family, and sorted through the various ideas floating around in my head. It might not have been the smartest thing to do, but I wanted to do it without having to look through e-mails in the morning.

What I also realized in these few weeks was that your ecosystem also starts changing with your change.

People challenge your dreams and conviction—people compliment me for being brave, but they also remind me about how many people have failed in such endeavors. You have a whole playing field to plot your game—my realization is that you could pick your position and pick your players. And you could decide when and where you want to play.

Professional friendships disappear quickly, but new refreshing friendships that come from unknown places emerge, and many of these people are in a similar situation as you. Risk-taking needs a lot of guts and self-awareness—this is real disruption. As you go about your day-to-day life, you are literally building everything from scratch. Things are super unstructured, and you need a lot

of clarity of thought and vision. You also need strong creden-
tials, high self-awareness, and a lot of positivity. And of course,
you need real money (the prospect of running out of money is
really alarming). Friends, family, and alumni come in handy—
and I have been fortunate to have good friends and family who
stepped up their engagement with me when I decided to make
this change.

Those first 8 weeks after quitting were good though. I got
time to think through my next venture. I got to spend time with
my family and my aging parents. I met with people who were
never a part of my networking ecosystem before. Above all, I
felt great as I worked toward the next thing in my life. I also
realized that the experiences from working in big companies are
valuable. I learned resilience. I learned how to do things big and
scale things globally. I got to work in different countries around
the world and understand the impact of culture. I learned how to
navigate complexity, which is a reality in any business. I learned
the meaning of failure and success in big companies. I learned
how to communicate, present, and drive impact and influence.

And I had the opportunity to work with countless wonderful people along the way. But I am also happy that I took the plunge.

For those of you thinking about changing your jobs, companies, or roles, I say, take the plunge, take the leap of faith, and self-disrupt yourself. The future belongs to self-disrupters if you know what you are doing. It is a lot of hard work as well. When you are settled in an existing job, it requires less work because of the familiarity and time that you have already spent on it. When you keep disrupting yourself, it takes extra bits of work to get up to speed before you disrupt yourself again. One a disrupter, always a disrupter. You need ownership, accountability, and conviction to do things. Above all, you need to be able to sense the roadmap ahead and have the conviction to make it happen.

Five

The Importance of Sensing

Look at the stars and not down at your feet.

Try to make sense of what you see, and won-

der about what makes the universe exist. Be

curious.

—STEPHEN HAWKING

Early 2000s in Singapore: We are sitting in a swanky conference room, overlooking the bay, doing a business review.
The view outside the window is stunning, and it caught my
attention more than the people in the room. I've always liked
Singapore because of the agility and adaptability shown by the
citizens of that small, resilient country. They are always making

changes, adjustments and improvements to keep their economy going, and they run the country like a corporation. At the same time, this is done in the backdrop of their culture so that their core social system stays intact.

In the business review, we are talking about creating a new channel ecosystem for the cloud business. There were several of us from different countries in Asia gathered for this offsite meeting. We had data, we had anecdotal examples, and we had a complete plan to talk about the opportunity. We were talking to senior leadership on this new business idea—people who had far more access to data and market conditions and knew more about the health of the business. And they were paid way more.

After several hours of discussion, our proposal to invest behind this new channel was rejected. Senior leadership said that that model would never mature, and this channel would never be able to scale to what other cloud providers could do.

That was incorrect. As the last few years have shown, the cloud channel ecosystem has undergone massive change and has become a critical part of the massive cloud-business opportunity today. It is a classic example of a couple of people who are closer to the market and customers sensing an opportunity faster. It is also an example of couple of other people missing the opportunity despite having more access to data and information. Unfortunately, if the latter happen to be decision makers, it is a problem for the organization.

I am sure this happens everywhere—it becomes a problem when this becomes endemic within an organization and sets in as the culture. People become risk-averse and primarily aim for survival rather than risk taking for new value creation. I am sure that people within Digital Equipment (DEC), Sun Microsystems, and several other larger organizations sensed the business change that was coming their way, but there was no way for the leadership to have been cognizant of that because they were too steeped in their legacy strategy that had made them successful in the past. Several years back, I used to work for Compaq (eventually acquired by HP) and worked on DEC systems—they were one of the best pieces of technology I have ever worked on. Along the way, a lot of people, including customers, realized that the DEC products were missing key trends and requirements to remain successful in the market, and they started moving elsewhere.

Eventually, DEC was acquired by Compaq and Compaq by HP, and most of their core technology was amalgamated into others. DEC was one of the best technology companies at that time, but it couldn't make it because of missed opportunities to keep pace with the market and customers.

The ability to sense is important in being successful in business. In Buddhism, there are six internal sense bases (*Pali: ajjhattikāni āyatanāni*, also known as organs) and six external sense bases (*bāhirāni āyatanāni* or sense objects; also known as domains). Thus, there are six internal-external (organ-object) pairs of sense bases: eye and visible objects, ear and sound, nose and odor, tongue and taste, body and touch, and mind and mental objects.

In essence, these pairs of sense bases are in use at all times. The mind's ability to quickly scan, translate into meaningful information, and then pattern match against an experiential or acquired knowledge base that can create the ability to sense. A lot has been said about leadership qualities and whether they are acquired or there at birth. The attribute of sense starts from the time we are born. It depends on our upbringing and the way people around us react to things. The difference between successful leaders and those who are not is the ability to sense early and quickly. And it is not just important to sense but to be able to translate that sense into action.

How do you translate sense into action that would be useful to an organization? You obviously cannot run up to your boss with every single idea that comes your way. You need to qualify the sense to make sure there is a degree of authenticity and practicality to the whole thing. We often dream things up based on what is top of mind for us from previous events or things we have read about or seen in a movie. They are all important influencers, but it's important to develop a methodical approach to self-validate and separate dreams from reality. Being able to process the sense is equally important as the sense itself.

I once had a bright person on my team who impressed me with his ideas. Then he had way too many of them. And once he was encouraged with one of his ideas, he thought he was the idea guru and started spending more and more time trying to think through junkie ideas to please me. Even if some of his ideas were good, they were hard to execute. It reached a stage where he started interrupting people during meetings, always coming up with a "brighter idea." It started messing with people's morale, and I eventually had to pull him out.

A lot of businesses fail when existing leaders lose the ability to sense. If you dig deeper, you'll find other people in those organizations who sensed the need for change but were not in a position to influence. I have spoken to many people in DEC who knew what needed to change but couldn't do anything about it. Sense needs to be nourished and nurtured to keep you ahead of the game. Sense is different from a hunch or gut feeling. You can do it on ongoing basis, and if you practice, it will happen automatically.

You can build strong long-term relationships through sensing. Once an employee came to me before a critical product launch saying that her father was not well, and she wanted to go see him the following week—which was when the launch event was, and she played an important role. In her mind, she was debating between going to see her dad then or later. I thought she should go. She made the trip, and we managed to hold her work together as per our plan. A few weeks later, her father passed away, and she was so happy that she made that trip. There are moments like this that come up at all stages of our business lifecycle—we need to sense them so that we are able to make the right decisions as much as possible.

Having done enterprise technology sales for a long time, I practiced hard so that I could sense deals. I could sense quickly whether it would be easy or tough to win a deal and how soon it would come my way. I was wrong that one time, when I was sitting outside the chief information officer's (CIO) office, waiting to sign a large technology contract. As my contract papers were getting printed, two people walked into the CIO's office. Their body language told me that something was amiss. An hour later, the CIO came out of his office and told me that these folks were from a group company, and they could do the same work we could at a lower price. He was obligated to sign them up, and we lost the deal. That one was really difficult to sense.

I have frequently ordered stuff online from Amazon, which saves me time, and it is easy for me to look through several things at once. To test the online experience, I ordered disparate things, last-minute gifts, books, shoes, and so forth, and my experience with Amazon has been consistent. When I tried the same thing with other online retailers, I haven't had a consistent experience. As I write this piece, I am waiting for a pair of shoes that I ordered through another online retailer that is already two days past its deadline, and I have no idea when it will get delivered. The online message says it is in transit, and the delivery date shown is two days earlier.

My sense is that it will be hard to beat Amazon in the online retail space. I agree that they are squeezing hard on margins, but customer experience really trumps everything else. I am sure Amazon has not always provided a consistent experience, but they are way ahead of the pack. They have a better way of managing the experience with a combination of technology and algorithms.

How do they do this? My guess is that Amazon has built inherent sensing into the business. If you look at several of Amazon's other businesses, you'll see the same ability to sense, the uncanny ability to almost predict a customer need or a market trend at the right time.

Seattle is also home to Starbucks, so I have to write about them as well. Ever since I quit my full-time job, I have been spending a lot of time at various Starbucks locations. Starbucks has become like my global meeting place. How I sometimes wish that they had conference rooms that I could book by the hour. Or a broader choice of healthy meals for lunch. Or an app that directs me to a less crowded Starbucks when I just need to just sit down with my coffee. I also think there is opportunity for Starbucks to promote and foster various kinds of startup (and student) communities.

It is important for business leaders to stay connected with the market and customers at all times. It is almost like we have multiple sensors that are always seeking signals, and the brain is processing them in real time. While I don't profess to be a guru in the art of sensing, it is a combination of our sense bases and how we use them on an ongoing basis.

Listening is probably the most important sense. When I am in important meetings, I just sit back and listen; and open up all my sense doors. While I listen, my eyes actively scan for any body-language indicators that tell me what is actually being said and what is being perceived (what the other person really means and what the other person does not). I let the energy flow in rather than letting my energy flow out through my talking. You can extend the concept of sensing in our day-to-day professional lives to almost any scenario. Heightened awareness to sensing can give you valuable pointers into your business and impact your survival.

Communication is another important aspect of sensing. People often sense things or see issues before anyone else; they have big ideas that others don't see. The problem is that they can't communicate or influence other people to see their points of view. Creators or sensors in many cases (especially in large, old organizations) stay quiet and don't challenge the status quo for fear of being pushed back on (fear of rejection).

Later in this book, I talk about several ways in which sensing can be encouraged. One can take the ability to sense to a certain level of predictability. You can use this to determine employee performance, motivation, and attrition; one can determine business performance usually way before others can.

There is an important element of sense in strategy and planning. The best MBAs and the best professionals churn out world-class strategies and business plans. Many of those plans do not see the light of the day because they lack the element of sense within. Sense is like the soul, the life, and the emotion inside the plan. The theory of 'empiricism' states that knowledge comes from sensory experience. While I am not saying that all knowledge comes from sensing, sensory experience plays a significant role in developing our belief and also influences our logical and reasoning powers.

I have sat through innumerable planning and strategy sessions in the various big companies I have worked for, sensing that many of these strategies and plans would not see the light of the day. Some companies have an approach of "disagree and commit". It means that everybody has to commit to executing on a plan even if some of them did not agree with the plan. This approach does not always work. Plans created without the soul are a waste of time, and even if people worked on those plans, a lot of them did not deliver desired outcomes. I have often seen plans get trumped by other plans, and people do not even have the time to measure the actual efficacy and outcome of the execution of a plan.

As we build teams, we need to include people who can sense. They can help save time, get us to market faster, remain competitive, and also set the stage for creating a vision for the project.

Where sense is wanting, everything is wanting.

—BENJAMIN FRANKLIN

Cloud computing is disrupting and transforming the technology business today. The potential is unlimited, and it is on its way to becoming a multibillion-dollar market opportunity that will impact every industry in the long run. Over the next ten years, a lot of people will move to the cloud, but it will not replace everything. Most customers are investing in multiple cloud technologies, and it is becoming a situation of having silos of cloud—like there used to be silos of technology before. Most chief technology officers are sensing this and are, therefore, hedging their bets into multiple cloud solutions. If you look at newer ventures, they are more in the cloud than big enterprise companies of the past. Some CTOs are ahead of the game here as they are accounting for different types of technologies that will have to co-exist in their environments for several years to come.

There is a lot of change in the education sector as well. For example, there is a shift to online training models. However, that won't necessarily replace on-campus and in-person programs. In fact, a combination works even better. While a lot of online education and training companies have come up, traditional colleges are sensing the need to make this change as well. Harvard Business School came to market with HBX, and the feedback has been positive. Some time back, I did part of an online course from Stanford University on machine learning that was extremely comprehensive and so well-paced that it could cater to students with different learning styles.

If you look at other industries like health care, automotive, or retail, you'll realize that a lot of transformation and disruption is led by technology. Rapid advancement of technology impacts business models in a way that now takes hours and days instead of months and years. It is even more important for leaders to develop the art of sensing because it will help them preempt challenges and opportunities and move faster. Over the next few years, every big company will be competing against a bunch of smaller, newer, technology-enabled companies that can sense better. Early sensing and risk taking will become the keys to survival and success in the new world.

Six

Survival versus Risk
Taking

Extinction is the rule. Survival is the

exception.

—CARL SAGAN

G rowing up in a socialist, democratic country with measured resources set the foundation for the initial years of
my thinking. It instilled a sense of accountability, resource management, and responsibility. It also instilled a sense of survival,
knowing what to fight for, what to live for and what to let go. It
created a strong desire for things that I eventually figured out
how to get. The flip side was that it didn't encourage a lot of risk

taking—for several years, I was risk-averse, trying to play the survival game to the core.

If you look at developing countries, you'll find, even today, that the core philosophy is one of looking for resources, accessing them, and figuring out ways to hold on to them. Developed countries, on the other hand, have plenty of resources, and their key philosophy is to distribute, consume, and reinvest resources as much as possible to generate new resources. In most developing countries, resources are limited, and people literally have to work hard to get them; hence, people want to hold on to them.

A lot of initial industrial and economic development in India was set with controlled and moderate goals; it was probably the need of the hour, given that resources were limited, and we had to cater to a billion people. My early growing up years in India set the foundation of my core philosophy.

Both approaches and environments (developed versus developing) create different aspects of sensing—the sense to survive and the sense to create. Both are important as we think of organizations trying to derive competitive advantage in the market, but, eventually, one takes precedence over the other. As you will read more about, sense to create prevails over sense to survive.

My exposure to things foreign started in my childhood, when several members of my extended family migrated to the United States (several decades ago). I still remember the chocolates, toys, airline first-class toiletry kits, clothes, that I got as gifts, whenever they visited India. That created desire, aspiration, and hunger for the finer things in life. I realized that I had to choose between being risk-averse to survive versus taking risks to -create more value in life.

Over the last few years, I have made several decisions that reflect a growing risk-taking behavior. I have changed my job three times when I was at my peak, twice when I had just been promoted to a higher level. Every time, I went in with more uncertainty and more risk, and, every time, I came out more successful and more enlightened than before. But it took me a long time to get there. I was always taught to survive and keep things going rather than taking chances and trying out something different. I wish I had moved faster and taken more risks early on in life.

The world is changing fast, and the rules are different. You need to take more risks than ever before and be hungrier than ever to achieve what you desire. Surviving in the new corporate world means adapting to the world of risk taking, which requires an innate combination of new skills, the ability to acquire knowledge rapidly, and a high degree of tech savviness, irrespective of the industry you are in. It also needs strong intent and that capability to sense.

About fifteen years ago, e-mail was hot. The technological advancement lifecycle used to be three to five years. Now, e-mail is passé and technological advancement is happening in days rather than years. I frequently come across senior managers in large companies who spend a few hours every day pushing e-mails, driving internal meetings to wait and watch, and trying to fight fires or solve SCIFI projects. Are they really adding value to the business? Are they really creating business impact that creates a competitive advantage and drives new net-value creation for the company? Probably not.

Newer generations and younger companies use more progressive technology and social tools to communicate and collaborate.

I find young kids (twenty-year olds) take several hours to respond to e-mails and are quicker on Apple or Facebook messaging and other social media tools. (I was recently told by some teenagers that WhatsApp is for older people.) In fact, some of these tools are so prevalent that they require a way to manage and handle them, or they can take over your life today. You need an ongoing strategy in your organization to adapt and adopt modern tools that are highly agile. This is where trade-off comes in between age-old systems and processes versus modern tools and outlook.

I was recently talking to somebody who was told by his company that he could not shop online on his office computer. Maybe he was spending a few minutes buying a gift for his girlfriend, but it was against organization policy. The lines are getting blurred between official usage and reasonable personal usage on office assets, but these will need to be figured out. This is not so much of an issue in modern companies where many people bring their own devices to work. Given the pace of technology changes, organizations who are able to adapt modern tools and technologies faster will be more agile and successful in the long run.

As I look back at the last two decades, the rate of change has quadrupled every three to four years. And the rules to survive and create are changing rapidly. The rate of value creation is also progressing at a rapid rate. Whether you are an established company or a startup, your need to create value in the same amount of time has grown multifold. You cannot achieve that through wait and watch, firefighting, or through SCIFI. Your leaders need to have the ability to sense and move faster to respond to and take action on ideas and opportunities. The underlying connective tissue for all of this is the ability to sense and to do it faster than others.

There are three phases of my life that have helped me understand and implement the concept of sensing. The first was my childhood in India when the Indian economy went from a controlled, socialist economy to a more open global economy. Those were the days when technology was mainframe computers filling up giant rooms. (IT used to report to the CFO in many companies—my dad was the chief accountant of a large multinational manufacturing company and the IT team reported to him), and punch cards were used for attendance in factories.

In those days, a lot of stuff was restricted in India like media, luxury goods, perfumes, fine chocolates; there was no concept of credit rating, and credit cards were not prevalent; color television was a luxury. I grew up watching black and white television and one fixed program everyday. E-mail and Internet was just getting started, and people used to share computers. Several food items were rationed, and families received a fixed quota every month through ration cards that doubled as IDs. The only foreign products we saw at that time were "localized" products by Unilever, Ponds, Cadbury's, and a few others.

By the time I was through middle school, the economy started opening up, and we saw transformation in infrastructure and banking and the emergence of foreign investments and global companies. While it still wasn't easy to do business in India, it offered huge market potential, with a big middle-class population with growing purchasing power, a modern outlook, quality education, and a highly tolerant culture.

The second phase of my learning was when I worked across different countries and cultures in Asia. Getting to respect diverse cultures, understanding the impact of culture on performance, and how people worked and how business got done in different countries was a tremendous learning experience for me. From the super-efficient Singapore, to the massively growing China, to a highly developed South Korea, I got valuable lessons on creation and survival.

Singapore is an example of high-efficiency survival and creation—happening at the same time. For the twenty-five or so times that I have gone to Changi Airport from wherever I lived in Singapore, it has always taken the same time whether it was raining or there was a road closure or an accident. At the same time, Singapore continues to invest in creating new initiatives to attract tourists and investors. It is one of the best examples of such coexistence anywhere in the world—feasible because it is a small country that is run extremely well.

China continues to amaze me with its industrial value-creation capability and how fast it does it.

South Korea on the other hand is a highly matured economy in Asia with a balanced focus on survival and value creation. It has big, stable corporations that produce wonderful things and are competing with hundreds of smaller companies in the world that are more agile in creating higher value, faster.

I have been to Amsterdam several times and am very impressed with the professional Dutch culture that I saw. It is easy to work with the Dutch; they are focused, honest, and transparent.

In Germany and with Germans, I saw the structured approach to everything. It is a highly developed and mature economy that is sensing opportunities and creating value at a rapid pace.

One time I was on a cloud-computing panel discussion in Jakarta when the panelists suddenly switched to Bahasa (the local language), and I had to quickly figure out how to get back into the discussion. It took me a while, and I had to jump back in without a logical connection to the previous comment because I did not understand what was said.

When I was in an important partner meeting in Beijing, the language changed to Mandarin in the middle of the meeting, and I didn't know what was discussed till we all met for dinner to celebrate the deal that was done.

Did I miss something here? These are examples of cultural forces that play in your immediate ecosystem, and you have to know how to maneuver across those to be able to create new value. At the end of the meeting, the most I could do was agree to what was broadly discussed by the others.

How do you handle such situations? The simple answer is you get into more of these situations, understand the local dynamics at play, and work through them. Learning from the hose is the best way to learn, and the more you do it, the more adept you get. I always tell aspiring business leaders to live and work for a few years in countries and cultures where they were not born. The perspectives you get are better than what you learn from any business school.

The third phase of my life was when I moved to the United States and managed several aspects of a global business. The scale, operational efficiency, strategic thinking, high social maturity, and organizational values are very different. The United States has such strong fundamentals and a stable social system that makes the overall business and economic environment attractive. One has to spend far less time in the United States managing work hygiene (basics of day-to-day work), which frees up quality time to focus on important work. The quality of life and the quality of education, freedom of speech, respect of people's opinions, and support for diversity are some of the amazing tenets that come naturally in the Western world.

But there is more. People living in America create social and economic value on a day-to-day basis. The projects that I worked on in Asia were super strategic and important. The projects I came across in the United States were strategic, cutting edge and high impact.

My appetite to take risks and work on bigger things went up in the United States. Survival continues to be the most important human requirement. But risk taking will take you to greater heights and create differentiation from the other strong performers around you. Risk taking is what will enable you to live your dreams and bring out the best in you. And if you can sense better, you can move faster and more accurately.

It is also important to be able to distinguish between right sensing and wrong sensing. An overzealous person can be over-sensing opportunities or ideas. There has to be a rational balance to calibrate the level of sensing required. This is a function of culture and right hiring. If you have hired the right people who believe in the organization vision and embody the culture, there are fewer chances of failure.

Culture is a combination of two factors—setting the culture and implementing it broadly. Setting culture is all about reinforcing, clarifying, and communicating broadly across the organization. Implementation is successful when grassroots people (other than the leaders) believe in and practice the culture that the leaders profess. The latter usually makes companies fail or succeed. The ability to sense is one outcome of cultural execution.

The environment also shapes your sensing abilities. People who are observant and exposed to different environments and cultures demonstrate a broader spectrum to sensing. If culture promotes openness, dialogue, and a genuine interest in new ideas and models, it will drive more engagement across a broad swath of the organization. I have several friends who have lived in different places as they grew up—I have found them to be more amenable to change, diversity, perception, and sense. Similarly, I have several friends who have never lived outside a single city for their entire lives—I have found their perspectives to be narrower than those who have lived in different places. This is a generalized statement and may not be statistically true, but I have seen this across the people I have interacted with.

I always encourage people to travel to different countries whether it is to vacation, study, or work. The experiences are invaluable and create a world-class citizen and leader within you. I came across so many people who work part-time to harness their passion for the rest of the time. There are more startups in the United States and Israel than in the rest of the world—because people believe in risk taking. In the United States, there are people from different parts of the world who migrated here at different stages of their lives. The environment and culture nurtures a unique risk-taking ability to enable people to sense opportunities (faster) and encourage people to take risks. Organizations can create such environments to foster ideas and opportunities and growth.

I had tried three times in my life to get to the United States because I was impressed with the opportunity that exists here from what I saw from my family who used to live here. The first time was when I was studying engineering. I had done an extensive college search for colleges (helped by my aunt) and was all set to take the GMAT/GRE exams. However, I was unable to move forward for financial and family reasons. If I look back at what happened then, I realized that I did not try hard enough and was not ready to take risks.

The second time was when I was working with Intel. I did not land the right opportunity, and I believe I did not try hard enough. The third time (lucky, but initially unplanned) was with Microsoft (a great company to work for if you want global business experience). When I finally moved to the United States, I realized that I had already changed from being a survival geek to a risk-taking nerd. A lot of this was shaped in the work I did across different countries when I was with Microsoft.

I was always a solid performer, so hard work and performance were never issues with me. The key was risk taking that I finally mastered as I worked with different people and cultures. I also realized (and it took me a long time to get there) that the world is full of survival geeks. The only thing that differentiates solid performers from people who start lagging behind is risk taking.

My best engagements, projects, and performances were when I took risks.

As I started looking at big organizations, I realized that I was increasingly surrounded by survival geeks. As people grow older, they get into the pattern of holding on to what they have and protect their bases. The more I grew, the more such people I found around me. And it becomes really hard to differentiate yourself within a bunch of survival geeks. That is when you need to stop, sense, and start again.

STOP

When I quit my last job, my wife wasn't working, and we had reserves to last us for a year. I had a kid in school and parents to support. What the heck—if we have to self-disrupt, might as well do it now. What happens if I am not successful in pursuing my dreams? We will figure out something else that works.

Belief and willpower are important to support your decision. I had a great supportive manager who told me to take a leave of absence for a few months to go figure things out. I had to disrupt myself so I had to *stop*. I said, "No. I want to quit and work things out the hard way." You need to stop and signifi-cantly disrupt yourself if you want to massively change course in your life.

START

I did not stop to retire. I did not stop because I wanted to start all over again. I sense there is so much more to do. There are so many opportunities that you cannot address in bigger compa-nies. Even with all the transformation and change, they are still slow, and they take time. I wanted to move faster and decided to take the plunge. To avoid a situation of fools rushing in where intellectuals fear to tread, your risk has to be calculated. There are four things that you must look out for when you get to this situation.

BELIEF

You need to believe that you can sense well and that you have a dream. I have seen numerous situations where good ideas have been brushed aside by more seemingly confident people, pri-marily because of lack of belief by the person who sensed the opportunity. Belief is a function of knowledge and awareness and can overcome false confidence. Belief will also help you go deeper into the situation and take calculated risks quickly. Belief may not inherently lead to better sensing but will definitely help you position and push your ideas.

CHANGE

There are two types of people—those who love change and those who hate change. This might not be a fair representation to the broad change-management spectrum, but I have realized you can classify most people into one of these two categories. Openness to change is inherent to sensing and, therefore, risk taking. Almost every sensing opportunity or value-creation activity will result in the need to change or the need to make changes. A person's comfort with change or change management will determine how the mind responds to change. So someone who loves change and wants to try new things will have a better ability to sense. Those sensing abilities will thrive in an environment that promotes risk taking and value creation.

NORTH STAR

It is important to have a north star, a source of inspiration in life. Dreams are led on by your north star and are nourished and nurtured along the way. This is like the energy and the force that keeps driving you toward your goal. Every time you sense something, you move closer to your north star.

I remember a leader I once worked for. Whatever business pressure we were under, I always came out highly energetic and passionate after meeting with him. Great trait of a leader in motivating and inspiring his team. However, I lost the spark within a couple of days of meeting him. I would be less inspired and less of a risk taker. I realized that his engagement with me was not sticky enough. While he was a good person and a great motivator, he was not helping me with a true north star to drive long-term business goals and sticky value creation. Longevity is, therefore, important when we think of a north star or a source of inspiration.

I once had a mentor in India—the best mentor I have ever had and a perfect example of a north star. He was always more prepared for the mentoring discussions than I was. In my second meeting with him, he succinctly summarized everything we had discussed in our first meeting. I hardly remembered anything. It was embarrassing, but I learned so much from him. I always aspired to be like him. He sensed things faster than I could realize. He sensed business opportunities and market conditions very quickly. Above all, what he told me stuck with me. He was full of belief, energy, and willpower to take risks to get to his dreams.

My uncle, Syamal Gupta deserves a special mention here. An alumni of Imperial College, London and Harvard Business School, he is a true example of a north star, a leader who could sense the future. He moved through the ranks of Tata Sons, a large business conglomerate in India. He was on their board and chairman of several Tata companies. He was passionate about technology and alternate energy, so he worked hard to get solar-power based green energy solutions and high-performance computing and other technology initiatives into India, when people were just starting to understand the value of these solutions.

WILLPOWER

You need tremendous willpower to drive things. At times of change, there is a high level of ambiguity, and only internal willpower can propel you through. There are many of us who want to go to the gym and work out every day, but we end up not doing it. I know people who have driven to the gym, parked, sat in their cars, and then come back from there. I know there are people out there who are highly talented but lack the willpower to take risks and do something. Willpower is like the motivation that comes from inside you so that you don't need an external force to motivate, drive, or push you.

I have always had tons of willpower—whether it was giving up smoking in a jiffy, giving up alcohol or whether it was pushing hard for that deal to close and going the extra mile to get something done. When you believe in something, never give up. This is not willpower to survive or hang on but willpower to take risks and create value. This willpower needs to be strategic, operational, and emotional to enable you to take the right calls in life.

You will find examples of several great leaders around you who demonstrate these attributes. Surrounding yourself with such leaders will help create an electromagnetic field of high energy that will keep you going. Whenever I meet with somebody, I either come out energetic or bored. If I'm bored, I never meet that person again. I'm sure the same thing happens to the people I meet; they come back to meet with me only when they find things to be energetic.

We find sticky inspirational people in sports, business, writing or politics, among other fields. Most of these leaders have had an uncanny knack for sensing opportunities and taking risk to live their dreams. Most of what they did had long-term stickiness as well. We remember scores of leaders who have shown grit and willpower to change things (we hardly remember people who kept status quo), and they have all made history.

Do we want to be such leaders in organizations who people will always look up to (Jack Welch, Bill Gates) and are sticky over the long run? Such leaders drive risk taking and value creation way more than the status-quo leaders. And they all had amazing sensing capabilities to build organizations and business models that last a lifetime.

Seven

Data Rules the Modern
World and No Backup Plans

Experts often possess more data than

judgment.

—COLIN POWELL

A few years ago, I was part of a team presenting a proposal to re-engineer the overall IT landscape and data-center strategy for one of our customers. We had done significant homework on their landscape and their business goals. Halfway through the meeting, the customer started pointing out flaws in our proposal. Our assumptions on their server utilization were not right. Our perspective on how much they could save was not accurate. Even our estimate of their capacity requirement was not what they were looking for. It ended up being a bad discussion, and we felt relatively stupid at the end of the meeting.

Despite all the preparation, we had not looked at the data properly. There were a lot of data points that the customer shared prior to the meeting, but we were not savvy enough to pull the right insights from that data. We lost that deal, and that meeting changed my life and my outlook on data.

Today is a world of data. There is nothing better than being able to corroborate what you sense with the data you have. There is a lot of data available. There is science in how you capture data, how you process data, drive pattern recognition, and use data to make decisions. If I refer back to one of the bad meetings of my life (elsewhere in this book), I went to a mentor afterward to ask how I could have handled that meeting better. The answer was data—data usually trumps a lot of hypothesis and creates a way of proving which ideas will work. If I had used enough data, I would have been able to qualify some of the hypotheses that were going around the room that day.

Become a data fan if you aren't one today. You cannot survive without data in the new world. If you don't like data, kiss running a meaningful business good-bye. I see people who shy away from getting their hands dirty with data and getting their finance or operation folks to look through data and provide insights—this does not work either. You have to be hands-on with data in your business. You need to love data, make love with data, and create the right insights that only a business leader or a middle manager like you can create.

It is really important to make sense out of the data. There is simple data and complex data; structured and unstructured data; and small data, big data, and more data. In the world today, where everything electronic can generate data, and we have Internet of things (IOT) going mainstream—we need to know where and how to get data and the rules to run on top of them.

There are numerous examples of how data can drive more effective business decision-making. As business leaders, the leverage you have from data is tremendous. You are closer to the business and, therefore, able to interpret data like no one else.

Today, one can generate data out of soda-vending machines and connect that with supply chain and fulfillment. Different sensors and software can help with predictive maintenance of mechanical devices and manufacturing operations. There are intelligent cars that will become even more intelligent and supply a ton of data as we connect across the value chain. Building automation and energy management systems will become more prevalent in households. Rapid advances in health care will drive a more-connected life experience. Retail will reach new heights where stores can target shoppers with specific offers and dynamic pricing. These will affect the business you are in even if you are not in the technology business.

One way to take risks and stay ahead without being overtly brash is by using data. Insights gathered from data can help you validate your sense and ideas to lower the risk.

Several years back, I was sitting with this customer in Asia when they had a tax raid in their offices. The tax officers did nothing except get to the IT room and lock it down. Over the next few weeks, they looked through volumes of data files and found that everything was in order and that there was nothing wrong with the operations of the company. Later, when I was talking to the CIO, he mentioned how disciplined they were about managing, protecting, and storing data within their premises. Their business model generated a lot of data and the fact that they were able to manage and process that data quickly saved them a ton of problems with the tax department.

It is not enough to have data. You need to pull insights from the data, and those insights need to drive action. Several times, I have made the mistake of sharing lots of data without specific insights and actions. I almost always got no response back, and I used to wonder why. You need to go the extra step with data. You need to drive insights and actions based on data. Data will change the world, and whoever owns or understands data will call the shots.

Don't become the old-boys' club on data. Data is not the work of the finance, Business Intelligence team, or data scientists in your organization—it is our collective responsibility.

Basic technology theory states that data needs backup. In fact, the more data you have, the more backup you need. The reverse might be true in business when it comes to backup plans. I used to have one or two backup plans for important projects in my life. It made me a highly successful project manager who never failed in different projects. But it also stopped me from going the full way in a lot of opportunities. I would switch to an alternate path during the life cycle of a project to ensure it didn't fail. This went on for a while, but I started reducing my dependency on backup plans. As of now, with the exception of a few projects where I cannot fail, I do not create backup plans any more.

Over a period of time, I realized that I have been more successful the few times when I have not had a backup plan. In fact, I started failing more when I had a backup plan. I know that we need to move fast and fail fast, but this was different. The fact that I had a backup plan effectively acted as insurance to failure and was completely counterproductive to risk taking. I spent more time creating backup plans than following through on the core plan. Back up plans impact value creation and risk taking— and while you will need backup plans for critical things, to be successful, it is important to have one primary plan that you bet your life and soul on.

We were working on an important project with a transportation company several years back. We created a great solution to manage the infrastructure operations. Halfway through the project, we were told that a couple of components of the solution would get delayed. True to the spirit of backup plans, the whole team decided to switch to a different solution with a new set of components. We were quick to make the switch, and everybody was happy because we were on track to deliver the customer's project. At the time of deployment, we realized that the new solution (which was the backup plan) had a fault in the architecture that nobody had validated because it was supposed to be a backup plan. We had to revert to the original plan and the project was delayed by three months. This was more than the delay in the shipment of the original missing components, which was six weeks. Backup plans sometimes work as quick fixes to problems that stop people from going the extra mile.

For a long time, having a backup plan was part of my DNA. Whether it was project work in school or getting a job, a customer contract, or a launch event, I was always ready with a backup plan. Life was smooth as I could quickly switch things around when something seemingly went wrong with my first plan. I sometimes had more than one backup plan for things, and I somehow always figured things out and work never got out of hand. Whenever something started to go wrong, I switched to a backup plan.

Later, I realized it was wrong. There are some mission-critical projects that need backup plans. But the approach of having backup plans stopped me from going the full way in a lot of opportunities. I pulled the plug and switched to an alternate path during the life cycle of a project to ensure it did not fail. I might not have given enough time to the original plan to succeed. I have spoken to several people, and I have come across quite a few who do this too. In their minds, there is always the notion of backup/recovery going on. Eventually, it takes over your life. At times, backup plans can be detrimental to core strategy.

How do you decide when you need a backup plan and when you don't? You need to sense the roadmap ahead and you need to sense when you need a backup plan. If you are working in a high-pressure situation, you definitely need a backup plan. When you are working on an established business project, you need a backup plan because you don't want to bring the whole house down. When you are working on a newer idea or taking a risk, you will have to go the full way on your desired path before you switch to a backup plan.

The thing that will help you decide is data. Early access to data will tell you if the valve in your assembly line will fail faster than before and if you need a replacement. It will tell you if soda bottles in a specific vending machine will run out faster than the others so that you can replenish the stock. Data will also tell you about the health of the car that you are driving way before anything goes wrong with it. Data coupled with sensing will help you get a sense of future situations and the roadmap ahead that can create actionable outcomes.

Eight

Middle-Manager Potential

A CEO's performance is as good as the perfor-

mance of his middle managers.

—MED JONES

I was a middle manager for several years in my career. In my mind, the middle manager is like the backbone in an organization or the wick in a candle—it runs through the middle of the candle and holds all the wax together. The role of the middle manager is important but can be ambiguous at times.

From a top-down perspective, they are meant to translate and implement decisions of the senior-leadership teams. Some of them are highly empowered and are able to make business and people decisions themselves. There are others who are good at doing what they are told to do.

From a bottom-up perspective, they are meant to represent the employees in their teams and protect their interests. They are meant to encourage risk taking and bring new opportunities to the business.

There are capable middle managers in different companies with aspirations and potential to go big. However, a lot of them retire as middle managers. Sometime back I did an analysis of middle-management leaders in a specific role—about one hundred people working in different companies around the world. In a span of over four years, none of those hundred people had moved up to take their leaders' jobs. Some of them left their companies and went to middle-management jobs in different companies. Most of them stayed on in their current roles, and some of them moved to parallel roles. It almost seemed that middle managers couldn't move upward. There were few examples of planned career shifts, progression opportunities, or developmental plans. Many of them were just stuck in their careers, unable to chart clear paths for themselves. Some of them were highly capable and rewarded, while others had already reached the pinnacles in their careers.

Middle management plays an important translation layer in big organizations and should take highest accountability for activation. Middle managers are the cultural backbones of the company. They need to buy into the company vision and strategy, and then percolate it through the organization. A lot of sensing happens at this layer, because these managers are sufficiently strategic to see the big picture and sufficiently operational to understand what is happening in the market with customers.

An organization will not be successful in sensing if its leaders are not good at activation, especially middle managers. That is why most of the times, companies miss acting on critical business insights, because downstream employees might have sensed it, but middle managers might not have activated it. Organizations need to think of continually empower and grow middle managers so that they can be more effective.

What should middle managers really be doing? Be bold in negotiating up—this is less about managing up and more about negotiating up. Get the right resources and projects from your team, and get the best investments. Empower the team and not be a micromanager—one of the repeated complaints I have heard from people is micromanagement by middle managers. Micromanagement stresses people out, and it does not bring out the best in them.

Encourage people to sense and take risks while staying compliant—don't restrict people to the strict boundaries of their jobs. Let them think beyond the box. Help people build careers and live their dreams rather than do their day jobs. Make the work environment a place that helps people take risks and work on what inspires them on a daily basis. Clarify relevance of their work to the company goals—I have heard from a lot of people, that they are unsure how their work contributes to the bigger strategy. Middle managers are best positioned to clarify such situations and keep the energy flowing.

Middle managers need to be balanced in their approach and need to amenable to different environments and operating conditions. In some sense, they are on a razor's edge. I have seen over aggressive and overtly bold middle managers get burned quickly because they are fighting too many battles. At the same time, the quiet ones are usually not heard, and they are more of the survival kind.

Middle managers need to be able to use the right amount of pressure, balanced with senior leadership. They definitely must be trustworthy and have spines to stand up.

One of my first customer engagements in India right after I graduated from Engineering was an educational Institute. We were working on a technology evaluation proposal with this customer. I was unhappy with the way things were going because I was looking for more transparency and information in the whole process (remember, I was fresh out of school). One day I called my manager and shared my frustration. He suggested I think it through and communicate what I thought was going on to the institute. Instead of thinking more, I wrote a letter and dropped it off at the dean's office, there and then. My manager called me later in the evening to say that the dean was upset and had escalated the matter to the CEO of our company. I did not know what to do. But, as a middle manager, he had my back.

We went back and apologized to the customer and also explained why we did what we did. The matter was resolved, but my manager lived through all the responsibility of a middle manager. He empowered and encouraged me to make the right decision in this situation and then he stood by me and negotiated with the senior leadership when matters went out of hand.

An organization needs to invest in such middle managers. They should be empowered to take risks, challenge the status quo, and invest on new opportunities. They should be positioned in less of a middle-man (man as in short from manager) position and more as aspirational leaders to run businesses or companies. We need to groom and grow middle managers with the right leadership roles and create development plans to overcome their gaps. Not every middle manager will progress to become the next level leader, but it will create a north star that middle managers will look up to and will provide a path and a challenge for middle managers to aspire to reach. Some of them will make it, and some of them won't. Either way, they will love the journey and learn a lot in the process.

Nine

Engaging People

ENGAGE

Whatever I engage in, I must push inordinately

—Andrew Carnegie

A couple of years ago, I was on a flight from Paris to Seattle and happened to be sitting next to a senior research physicist who worked with the Bill & Melinda Gates Foundation. Since I was working with Microsoft, we ended up chatting quite a bit, although our areas of work were totally different.

He was engaged and excited in his work, and he talked about how things could move really quickly in the foundation. One time, he submitted a research proposal on a Friday, and he got approval from Bill on the following Monday. He was new to the foundation, and it was totally unexpected for him because proposals like these took weeks or months to mature in other places. He was delighted at the pace and how the foundation picked his project for funding. It created a tremendous sense of engagement and energy with the foundation, with him. I could sense it in the way he was talking. This is an example of people engagement and the fact that energy revolves around people more than products or services. It is the human face of the company that drives most engagement.

Employees' engagement with an organization is not determined just by compensation but by the energy and involvement they demonstrate in their day-to-day life. Our human resource practices should be more about driving people engagement and culture so that people feel inspired to get to work every day and are super passionate when they talk about what they do. They need to show the human face of the company.

Once leaders have sensed opportunities or problems, the next critical step is what they do about it. This is what we call engagement. Leaders cannot do everything themselves, and it is important to have supporting people and teams that can help understand and execute on the sense that the leaders had. Things have to move fast from thereon. Many times, downstream employees are able to sense things faster because they are closer to the problems, and leaders are surrounded by people who don't sense those opportunities. I have seen numerous instances of solid opportunity sensing being shot down by pure political bullshit or incompetence.

There are times when this sensing by downstream employees is accurate and worth an evaluation or engagement. This becomes an issue since leaders tend to ignore downstream sense coming up to them. This is because they have blinders on; have created a wrong sense of self-awareness about themselves; or their styles are WAW, PASS, or SCIFI and prevent them from comprehending new opportunities.

Before we go deeper into people engagement, I want to spend some time talking about people practices. A lot of companies have under-empowered human-resources (HR) leaders and HR business partners. Many of them are under cost pressure (especially in low-margin businesses) that tends to reduce focus on people development.

A lot of people processes in bigger companies are old, and there is a huge gap in calibration with new-age companies. Some of those exist because of cultural and business-model differences, but, in general, people process need to change and modernize with time if you want to hire and retain the right talent.

People development is about more than recruiting, compensation, working hours, and holidays. Yet most people I have talked to remember these as the top HR functions for their company. HR plays an important role in driving people strategy and translating the meaning of organizational culture to employees to bring in a level of trust and consistency in the way they do it. Like I referred to earlier, talented people take jobs because of the opportunity, the manager and the culture they bring more than the compensation they provide.

First, HR needs to help hire (not just recruiting but also onboarding) the right people. It is important for HR leaders to understand the business and be part of the business. That is the only way they can help hire the right people. That is the only way they can understand business issues and roadblocks to help bring the right talent to an organization.

Over the last few years, I got interview calls from several technology companies for different jobs. The most interesting engagement was with Amazon where a specific recruiter was able to clearly articulate the vision of the group or the business over a sustained manner over a period of time. He knew when to bring in functional business people for a follow-up discussion. And he knew what I wanted and would pitch the right opportunities to me. I have tried to emulate this thinking in my hiring practices. Whenever I work with HR people, I first update them on my business and make sure that they understand my goals and objectives. It is important to look at the people function within the framework of the business.

The second aspect is to be able to retain and develop talent. Talent-retention efforts in many companies are inconsistent and essentially targeted at senior leadership. For the rest of the organization (especially in traditional organizations), talent management is about performance calibration rather than talent retention. There is limited veracity of succession slates, and professional-development plans are virtually nonexistent. There are some leaders who drive their own approaches within a large company, but this creates inconsistency and leads to frustration among employees of different groups.

CEOs need to hire strong HR leaders who can embody their vision and strategies and be the chief people's officer in the company. I spoke to several people on HR practices in big companies. The feedback I got was that HR is active behind the scenes and does a lot of good work, most of which is not visible to the rest of the organization. Is there a way we can create more visibility for the work done by HR that can help build more trust within organizations? In addition to hiring and retaining the best talent for the company, HR needs to create an environment of trust, high energy, and risk taking. You don't want low-energy people to walk in the door every morning and walk out the door in the evening. How do you build an environment like this? I asked business leaders from several companies to give me ideas. One was that HR leaders should come from the business. Being business centric will make them understand the nuances of business, which can help them hire and retain the best talent. Another idea was that HR should work closely with business leaders to formulate key people *and* business decisions.

There was unanimity on the fact that HR leaders should overcommunicate and establish trust and openness by engaging with people at all levels in the organizations. Take the pulse of the business by having lunch with a few people and listen to what they have to say. If there is a pattern, dig deeper and figure out what's happening.

Most people want HR to drive standardization and consistency across large companies, which is a difficult task to undertake. One of the things that demotivate employees is lack of consistency across organizations. This is not consistency of compensation but consistency of implementation of policies and benefits. What becomes even more painful is when leaders are aware of such situations but are unable to make any constructive changes. Consistency is a key element in building a trustworthy and risk-taking environment in any organization.

Sensing depends a lot on the environment. How many times have you walked around an office and felt like sharing or discussing an idea with somebody? It comes to you for a few minutes and is gone by the time you're in your next meeting.

I recommend that companies set up online sense pods through social networks where people can share thoughts and ideas. You can also set up sense boards where anybody from within the organization can record an idea or thought. This is a conceptual idea—it doesn't have to be as structured, but what I am recommending is a platform where people can ideate on an ongoing basis. Several organizations have periodic events and forums to share such ideas, but the structure of the event kills creativity. Keep it free, let it happen any time, and listen to it. Keep track of the pulse.

These sense boards and sense pods can be anonymous or not, and anybody can look through them. Peers, colleagues, or leaders can look through them and get more sense out of the same ideas that the originator might not have had. They can then add to the idea. When there is sufficient weight behind an idea, it is definitely worth evaluating for the business. This also breaks the traditional model, where rank and authority determine opportunity and creativity. This is one way to keep engaged with employees on an ongoing basis.

One of the frequent complaints I have heard from employees in large organizations is that it is really hard for them to meet with senior leaders and decision makers. Most structured events with leadership teams are so regulated that there is limited scope for an open discussion, especially for people who are quieter. I have been to several team meetings and leadership events where half of the room is busy shopping online, playing games, or checking e-mails, unless there is a highly inspirational speaker. Walk around the back of a reasonably large room where a structured event like this is going on and somebody is presenting, and you will know what I mean.

When I used to work in offices that had open cubicles, we could get up and talk to people, walk across, and get our work done. When I started working in offices that were closed rooms, I got restless sitting on my own in the office so I walked around and tried to get into other peoples' offices (if they were not busy) to strike up a quick conversation or discuss an idea. It was hard, as people were protective about their spaces, and I felt like I was doing a cultural intrusion. Later, one of my teammates told me how much he appreciated my walking to his office and talking to him—that helped him get answers to quick issues without having to set up a meeting. He said his previous manager of four years had never once walked into his office for an informal chat. Every decision for him was by e-mail or through a meeting.

The idea of creating an environment for people to sense opportunities is like crowd sourcing creativity. You take away the power and responsibility of creativity and ideation from the business leaders and give it to the masses. You create an environment, and let your people do the rest. If you have hired and retained the right talent, it will do wonders for your organization. Every business, every industry is different, so you will need to customize your approach based on what works best for you. Obviously, when you crowd source you run the risk of getting way too many ideas, and not all of them will be relevant to the business. But you will have to take that chance, and it is better to get more than less.

There are various ways to find the top ideas from all the ideas you generate. A friend of mine runs a boutique consulting firm and positions himself as the chief ideas officer. He actively seeks and gets a lot of them from his team on an ongoing basis. He then assimilates those ideas and brings them up in his customer discussions. Based on feedback he gets from customers, he summarizes and routes the top ones to his team. The team iterates the top ideas for the business to hone and sharpen them.

The other thing to do is to calibrate new ideas against existing strategy. If my friend gets stuck with a problem or has a concrete new idea, he calibrates that against his existing strategy to determine the impact. This helps him create a fully rounded net-new idea, once that doesn't conflict or overlap with existing strategy. It is usually hard to drive engagement based on sensing, and you will likely get a lot of resistance. Some people will pass it off as gut feeling or anecdotal evidence that cannot be used to drive business—which is why you need to fully validate an opportunity with your customers and with data that you have.

Another friend of mine was launching new software. A few days into the launch process, he realized he was boxed into a standard template launch plan without having done anything. He had a lot of ideas and a lot of thoughts from what he was seeing in the market, but he was told that his best bet was to follow what has always worked. If he didn't follow the plan, he would be responsible for any disaster. He decided to take a risk and follow his sense—he changed everything. He cut down on the several initiatives that were planned as part of the launch effort and decided to go deep with a simple customer-use case-based launch effort.

During the process he faced revolt, as not everybody bought into the new plan. People were unsure and uncertain about how things would go. He used a combination of persuasion and communication to get people onboard. He reduced the size of the launch team, and removed people who were not onboard with the plan from the team. He was immensely successful—he created a new launch process and got a lot of people thinking hard about how they could do things differently. This one action also set a new culture in the group—they started thinking more openly, started taking more risks, and started sensing opportunities. Sensing is a science of how our brain does pattern matching on what we sense in our day-to-day activities against our knowledge and experience.

The only way to make sense out of change is to plunge into it, move with it, and join the dance.

—ALAN WATTS

Another aspect of successful engagement is managing change.

I am a big fan of change and have always made bold moves in times of change. This has included changing jobs and moving from one country to another. I have made changes to business models and processes and adapted things along the way. However, there is another aspect of change that is equally important. I have come across leaders who, when they take on new responsibilities, make changes just to make their presence felt. Often, their idea of change is to change everything because there is something wrong with what exists today.

Sometimes you don't want your core strategy to change when you have a new business leader. I have frequently come across senior leaders in organizations where I have worked where adaptability means changing everything. Strategy changes with the leader. I have seen widespread frustration and discontent among employees when this happens.

I am usually wary when leaders come in and want to change everything. Are they asking the right questions to be able to make those decisions? Have they spent enough time understanding the market and impact of change on business and customers? Leadership change decision making is also dependent on the information leaders receive from their immediate teams. I have seen a situation where a team would recycle PowerPoint slides every time they needed to present to a new leader. The core content used to stay the same; the slides were tweaked to match the leader's profile and style and would always advise on status quo This was done by downstream teams of people to avoid changes to their franchise. The leader would end up not getting enough of the right information to be able to make meaningful changes to the organization. It reduces people engagement in the organization, results in loss of talent, and has long-term impact on the business. I have a list of five things to check when widespread changes to their businesses.

- Understand market challenges and opportunity clearly
- Have clarity on existing vision and where you want to go
- Solicit feedback from employees across the company
- Understand impact of change on the business
- Have a point of view on people strategy

These are principles of change-awareness that is important to consider in times of change. I have seen that many changes happen in a hurry without the necessary due diligence. Leaders do not have sufficient time or frameworks to land change so, thinking through some of these principles will come in useful. These principles look simple but you will be surprised how many times leaders are able to just look at one of two of these and make big change decisions.

'Wisdom starts with understanding yourself'.

—ARISTOTLE

Self-aware and sensing leaders are more effective in driving change than others. They will, in turn, drive more value creation than survival leaders. The other point to ponder is how much change should be driven top-down versus bottom-up. Are downstream employees and middle managers empowered to lead and drive organizational change? What can leaders do to have their teams lead some change initiatives bottom-up through the rank and file of the organization?

Change-navigation strategy is also important. One of the difficult meetings of my life was when I was transferred to a new office. I was full of zeal, and my boss called in sick on Sunday and asked me to attend a meeting on his behalf on Monday. I should have said no, but I said yes. I walked into this meeting, brand new to the office, hardly knowing people, with five senior leaders in the room. I started the discussion, and, within couple of minutes, lost control of the meeting. For the next fifteen minutes, the discussion was chaotic, and it became a battle of wits between the senior leaders. Tricky questions were asked, and the whole thing got complicated, as I didn't have many answers. We left the room achieving nothing. I cut a sorry figure for myself, and it took me a few weeks to repair the damage done.

I take the blame for this fiasco, but I learned a lot from this meeting. During times of change, it is important to calibrate the impact and make decisions accordingly. As I look back at the outcome of the meeting, I still feel bad for not having managed expectations and controlled the meeting. I hold myself accountable for the poor change management in this situation. I also went back and checked out all the hypotheses and decisions from that day. None of them saw the light of the day.

There was another notion that played out in the room that day. I call it management by hierarchy. The theory is that hierarchy leads to better business understanding and better business management. The discussion in that room had turned hierarchal. That is probably another reason we made less progress. Hierarchy is to ensure organization, teamwork, and motivation; you need different skills to run a business. You need to encourage employees to sense opportunities, engage, and work on them.

We need to differentiate between chief hierarchy officers and good leaders. Hierarchal leadership kills creativity and value creation, because leaders lead by hierarchal rules and fear-mongering. This style of leadership does not work by itself in the new world. This is why some newer companies are better equipped to deliver value than others. I'm not saying that you run a company like a jungle with no hierarchy: hierarchy is good to establish rules, code of conduct, financials, and so forth, but not to run the business or to foster creativity. There is a subtle difference here.

So what are some of the best practices of driving people engagement? We discussed a few earlier; here are a couple more. A few years ago, I was working on a business plan on new ideas for the cloud business. I was struggling to get stakeholders to see my point of view about the opportunity and the new strategy. I was super passionate about this business, so I went around sharing my views and asking other stakeholders if they could answer my concerns. During the process, I realized that they were not clear about my plan. I had not done a good job articulating my vision. It was important for me to recalibrate and start again. I had to share my vision and go through the execution plan in detail. I went back to the drawing board, reworked the plan, and started socializing the plan again. One by one, it was like hand-to-hand combat getting everybody on board.

Broad socialization of an idea or strategy that you have sensed is a good thing to do. It helps clarify your vision and the execution plan. It helps hone in on key stakeholders who can help execute later on. I have seen people who shy away from broad socialization—they create plans under the radar and push them through quickly, only to talk about them later. It is as much a networking and selling exercise as raising funds for your venture is.

The other approach I have seen people use is pre-socialization or back-channel socialization. I also do this at times. I reach out to key stakeholders on the side before key discussions to seek their views and buy-in. This helps garner support, and you get a sense of what works with those key stakeholders. You also get valuable input on potential gaps and weaknesses in your plan. This approach gives you enough time to iron out problems in your plan.

Once you have socialized your plans, how do you get broad engagement and commitment from people to execute on the plan? How do you drive energy and passion so that people bring their best to work? This is especially important in times of change when there is general uncertainty and doubt in people's minds. You have the usual tools to motivate and inspire people. However, instead of just doing this top-down, you can get coworkers and peers to do some of that.

I once had a team of seven people, where each person played a unique role to keep the team going. There was one person who was like the chief energy officer—always positive and full of energy. One person was like the chief provocation officer—always asking the right questions. Another person was an embodiment of engagement—understood strategy and was deep into execution. The other four people just followed these three. There were times when I sat in team meetings and saw how beautifully this played out. It was a small team, but it was surprisingly easy for me to run because the people played different roles. They sensed the right opportunities and created high-value and long-term sticky outcomes, one after the other.

The final thing I want to talk about here is pushback and the ability to say no. Push back, even if it is to your CEO or the board. Most of the time, we make wrong decisions because we cannot say no. It is even more difficult when these organizations are led by hierarchy or fear. I have been in senior-leadership meetings where a senior leader beat down the first question asked in the room and beat down on the person who asked it. No one ever asked any further questions, and nothing valuable ever came out of those meetings. It's also an example of how culture can be set and demonstrated at every single meeting.

I have seen how e-mails from CEOs or senior leaders have had different interpretations and implications for different people. There is the hierarchy mentality among employees where anything from the top is like gospel. I have seen situations where people leave everything and scramble to find an answer to questions from senior leaders. They never push back, even if they know there is something wrong. If you sense that something is amiss, push back. It is not fair to expect that leaders know everything—but if people don't tell them that, they will work on wrong assumptions that will do more harm in the long run.

Some leaders have what is a called a project-management office (PMO). Their job is to keep track of strategic projects and chase down people to follow up on their actionables. Noble cause, but most of the times I have seen the PMO become the cause and not the outcome (effect).

I was in this situation once when one of my projects came under the radar of a PMO. I sat through hours of meetings, looking at Excel spreadsheets, reviewing project details line by line. I felt less like a business leader and more of a project manager. The PMO becomes the pushback point, so your counterargument sometimes never reaches the leader because the PMO acts as a shield. Eventually, you end up spending so much time on project management that you lose track of where you started and lose touch with the business. They are like the chief orchestration officers I spoke about before—if they don't know the business well enough, they end up making wrong decisions.

There is a need to transform business practices and people engagement, tightly coupled with business transformation. If you want to drive good people engagement, empower them to work on the challenging opportunities, provide them with an environment that supports risk taking, and create a highly consistent culture that people can trust.

Ten

Activation

You have to lead people to get excited and be

passionate and be activated by what they do.

—TAYLOR HANSON

I have been working with a real-estate property agent for the last four years. She is not only honest, diligent, and knowl-edgeable, but she goes out of her way to get things done. For example, when we went to see a house, she came prepared with data on neighborhood properties that were recently sold and the market overview, even if I did not ask for it. Always prepared, already ready.

She kept showing us houses till we got to the one that we were looking and that met our needs 100 percent. She never once tried to shove a near match down our throats. She tried to get us connected to support teams from her organization even before we asked for it. An end-to-end delightful experience. She not only sensed what we needed, but she was superactivated to go above and beyond to support our requirement.

I have worked with other property agents in the past, and I can tell you that you don't get this everywhere. We were one of the several people she works with every month, but she made sure that our experience was highly engaging, and I'm sure she did that with the others as well.

In an organization, once you have people engaged and key stakeholders have bought into what you sensed and created, it is important to activate people to do something about it. This is important—like a workout at the gym. You need to activate a lot of your muscles to get the maximum out of your workout. The more relevant muscles you are able to activate, the better your body will function and the better the outcome of the workout. All the muscles in your body might not function at high potential all the time, but getting the most relevant of them working together is of utmost importance. And what ultimately matters is how your core performs.

Your organization is like your body—you need to know what muscles to activate at what point in time. Most importantly, you need to activate their cores. A leader is like a trainer—knows what to activate and what to train on at a point in time. Activation needs to be closely watched by bigger companies because non-activated people can fail companies.

I remember my days in a technology company in Asia in the early 2000s. We had bright professionals churning out strategy slides by the day. Most of those presentations did not see the light of day. I thought there was some amazing sensing going on in the company that people were engaging on, but there was no activation. The company had a lot of opportunities, but a lot of that was not getting activated. That company eventually recalibrated and got things to work and has become, and continues to be, an industry leader today. If companies capture the top ideas and opportunities that float around in the workplace, they might be in a completely different place from where they are today.

I remember an incident with one of my managers when I submitted my resignation. When I told him the reason I was leaving, which was the lack of activation in the workplace, he laughed and told me that I needed a change of environment. I should go work in a different office, and that would change my perspective. He missed the point completely. It was his environment that needed a fix. This shows how the manager was not able to sense what was happening in the organization, and he was asked to leave a few months later.

The other aspect of activation is motivation. Motivation is the key to success anywhere. Activation involves widespread deployment of the business plan and needs highly motivated people to do it. It is more than execution. It includes world-class execution plus going the extra mile to make the difference to your customers. This is a function of how well motivated your employees are. And that needs to happen consistently across the board.

Your experience with flying with an airline is a combination of experience with the ground staff, plus the in-flight crew, plus baggage handling, and other trivia that you are exposed to. I have been extensively following different airlines and how they are restructuring their strategies, but the one that rates high on my radar is Singapore Airlines. I have never had an inconsistent experience with them in all the times I have flown. Even their telephone-support staff shows the same quality as their ground staff. I have also had good experiences with Delta and their professional handling of people and operations.

The one place where many airlines fail is consistency. Sometimes it takes fifteen to twenty minutes to get to an agent when you call an airline. Some airlines have a problem with ticketing. There are some that make you feel like you shouldn't have boarded that flight. Few make it consistently across the entire customer-experience life cycle. The broader your customer-engagement spectrum, the deeper your need to drive consistent motivation across the life cycle is.

Here's a great example of strong execution but low activation. A couple of years ago, I was visiting Athens around the time of the financial crisis. As I went about talking to local people, went to local restaurants, and went through the city, I noticed a sense of low activation. Such a beautiful city, rich in culture and heritage, and with great food but impacted by economic problems.

The general feeling was that the government needed to do much more to activate the lives of Greeks, and they were unsure about what was happening and what they were expected to do. They were trying to figure out what was happening to improve the overall health of the economy, and they were hopeful. Some of them were engaged and activated, but others were waiting and trying to figure out where things would go.

This is relevant in business as well. People need to sense that they are activated and working on the right cause. You cannot create world-class organizations with just hope—you need highly engaged and activated people who are hopeful and optimistic. Activation plays a key role in creating successful companies.

There can be varying levels of activation in different parts of the same company. You can see these differences between various retails stores, coffee shops, health clinics, and so on. There are some Starbucks locations I prefer over others because of the high energy level and activation, which is not as consistent as their coffee.

The one company where I saw a high level of activation was Compaq—a computer company that does not exist today (it was acquired by HP). Prior to the DEC acquisition, all their muscles worked together in a consistent manner. There was a high ability to sense opportunities, engage, and activate in a company run by a highly energized Michael Cappellas. I even remember the internal communication process through periodic memos that

Cappellas started—which provided a sense of direction and activated people to do work over and above what they were required to do. Everybody was eager to jump in and help a new person joining the company as much as they would do with an existing employee. I know how excited and engaged the HR team was when they rolled out job offers to potential candidates.

If you look at companies like IBM with Gerstner, General Electric with Welch, Bill & Melinda Gates Foundation with Gates, Apple with Jobs—they are all super activated companies. You will notice the connection between the companies, their CEOCEOs, and their performance. There are hundreds of other companies I could call out that have the same level of activation that made them so successful.

In some ways, the activation agenda is laid out by the CEO. It is a key part of the culture-setting process in an organization. Activation requires that people share and collaborate broadly, be transparent in their work processes, and are highly energized to sense new opportunities. They are able to take risks to make these opportunities real for the business and to carve out new ways to do things.

In this modern world, you have to be agile. Activation demands agility. Agility might mean different things to different people, and sometimes it gets confusing. I hear people doing wrong things in the name of agility. Agility might be about doing things faster but may not all the time. It is about being able to sense customer requirements, and then being able to respond quickly. It is not just about doing things faster.

A few years ago, I met a customer after losing an important deal. I was keen to find out why the customer decided on a competitor when our solution was solid. He said that the reason was not the product or price but something else.

His first reason was that our company had five people working with his team during the evaluation process. There was a general lack of consistency and difference of opinion on how our solution would get implemented. There were varying levels of activation with the five people. Our competitor had just one person working with their team. He was a highly empowered and activated person who managed everything end-to-end and pulled in additional people from his side as required; however, he would always be responsible for the outcome.

His second reason was that we took an average of three to five days to respond to his team's queries, whereas our competitor would do it in a few hours (most of the time). According to him, this was agility. He decided to go with our competitor because of consistency and agility. These are all attributes of a high level of activation in a company. People take the effort to be consistent, collaborate deeply and be agile in responding to customers.

Consider another example of a typical software company. I come across several engineers trying to ship faster and get into faster release cycles. In one such discussion, I asked them if they had validated what they were doing with customers, and they said no. Doing things faster in the name of agility when it is totally unrelated to a customer need is not agility. Agility comes from sensing customer requirements quicker than others do and responding to them quicker than others do. The first part is sensing; the second part is activation.

Eleven

Learn and Lead

Live as if you were to die tomorrow. Learn as if

you were to live forever.

—Mahatma Gandhi

I am a big fan of ongoing learning. Some of it happens on the job, while some of it happens through structured tools and training. In today's world, one does not need classroom training sessions; online training works equally well. Given the amount of change and transformation that companies are going through, we need to encourage employees to undergo mandatory trainings. We have all heard the story of the exceptional sales representative who was a star performer year after year, and then something went wrong. He started failing, and when this happened for three consecutive years, he didn't know what was going wrong. He went to a coach who told him that his old sales techniques wouldn't work anymore, and he needed to upgrade himself.

Customers today are smarter about buying decisions because more information is available online. Whenever I get a chance, I train myself. Whether it is to go back to school at Harvard for a leadership program or an online machine-learning course, I keep learning on an ongoing basis. I trained myself on the job by being as hands-on as possible with the products I worked with. Knowing your customers, products, and competition is of utmost importance. Staying ahead of the curve by continuously updating yourself is equally important.

Learning is an important phase of the sensing cycle. New learning can be added to your knowledge base to make an even more intelligent decision the next time. The more you learn, the more your knowledge base grows, and that makes you a better leader.

Several years ago, I was actively involved in the election of a student-governing body at my engineering college. I came straight out of surgery for a perforated appendicitis (lucky to be alive), and I was passionate to improve the state of affairs at the college. This college had provided some life-changing experiences and sown the first seeds of risk taking in my life. A few weeks after the surgery, I went against one of my best friends at that time to put up and support a rival candidate for the post of general secretary of the student body. I knew I was on the wrong track with this one, and, at the cost of my friendship, we fought the election and lost. This was a great learning for me that I use time and again.

There are a lot of ideas out there, and you can sense a lot, but you need to pick the right ideas and the right battles. We need to sense the right battles, be self-aware of our capabilities, and be engaged and activated to run the full life cycle.

We were once working an important deal with a financial services customer organization deploying advanced technology solutions for their taxation systems. I was on point to deliver the critical technology presentation from our side, and we were the first of the four shortlisted companies for this purpose. However, we arrived late (darn traffic) and lost our presentation slot.

Not wanting to give up, we met with the project director and, based on our pitch, he decided to give us another chance at the end of the day if we were willing to come back. So we literally moved from the top spot to the last spot. This was a blessing in disguise. We anticipated that the customer would have sensed gaps with the solutions the other vendors proposed. In the ensuing time, we changed our entire presentation. When we presented our solution, we took a competitive stance, reminding the customer of how our solution was different from our competition. It was a simple situation but it worked for us.

I could sense the vibes at the point of time and knew that we would get the deal. We got the deal a few months later. Would we have lost the deal if we went in first? Maybe not, but we adapted our approach to inspire and instill confidence in the customer and that sealed the deal for us. We were told later that we showed a high level of energy and activation that got the customer to come to us. Since we went in at the end, we changed our approach on the fly, sensing what happened during the rest of the day. This is an example of a "sensetionary" approach. The whole team was engaged and fully activated on this deal. Guess what company we used to work for at that time—Compaq! I learnt a lot from this deal especially the importance of adaptability.

There are examples of different methods and ways that are set up to facilitate organizational learning, but people do not use them effectively. Learning is a combination of structured and unstructured knowledge. You can get structured knowledge through training programs, while you can acquire unstructured knowledge on-the-job or through online programs. I have undergone and facilitated several training programs. Structured learning programs in isolation do not work in the new world. I have seen people flip through content, get others to do their course-work, or leave halfway through. Even then, they get credit for those trainings, even though they were not really trained. So, learning has to be self-motivated and self-directed.

Seeking feedback and working on feedback is also an important part of learning. I closely watch feedback and survey requests. It is interesting to see that many have been repeating the same feedback form for years that does not keep pace with the changing environment I have also seen that many companies do not have a structured process of taking action on feedback. They would collect feedback and then use primitive tools and methods to review the feedback. One of the things we found useful is to refer back to feedback we received in every subsequent meeting. We used to run forums for partners where we reviewed and presented feedback from previous forums to show that we value feedback and that we also keep them updated on the progress. Whether it is employees or customers, they feel highly energized when they are heard and action is taken on their feedback. This is a great way to drive learning in an organization.

Learning needs to be an integral part of the engagement and activation process. You cannot start everything from scratch all the time. How do you use learning to lead and transform? One of the ways to drive more value creation for businesses through learning is to use the knowledge derived from ongoing learning to continuously adapt and improve business models. Does your organization allow you to do that?

I have sat through several leadership trainings that produce a lot of good ideas and knowledge, but most of it doesn't get used in future business practices. A lot of learning is essentially shelved at the end of the training. Organizations need to build flexibility into their business models to allow newer ideas to come in through various learning programs. There are different ways to integrate the culture of learning and leading into an organization.

Provide tools and processes for people to share their learning with organizations in a structured manner. Encourage employees to practice peer-to-peer learning.

Leaders should act as coaches or trainers rather than managers to absorb and implement outcomes from structured leaning.

We need to drive innovation in learning—it has to be self-facilitated and on-demand rather than a hard-line approach. In the new world, people will learn then they need to and when they want to not when they are told to.

People in different parts of the world sense, learn, and engage differently and even react differently to the same problem. This could be a function of demographics, upbringing, local culture, family influence, or business conditions. The nature of learning varies from culture to culture and we need to be open to accommodating learning from where it comes from and not just from where it began (the source).

Like everybody else, my learning started when I was in school. I grew up in a small town called Allahabad in Boys' High School.

As the name suggests, it was a boys' only school at that point of time. It was strict, highly disciplined and encouraged broad based thinking on core issues. Those days, even to attend a cultural program in another school, we had to take permission from the school management. The Indian economy was relatively closed those days, so there was discipline across the board – in learning, in spending and in living.

The economy opened up as I grew up. My initial learning created a sense of accountability, a higher degree of discipline, and a focus on value creation. When resources are limited, you have to do your best with what you have, and you usually won't get a second chance.

As the economy opened up, more goods and services became available, and you could literally buy anything if you had money. All of this had a huge impact on my learning, as the pendulum swung 180 degrees. Based on those years of learning I can apply socialist policies on one side to balance market-led demand/supply insights to solve business problems. This allowed me to look at problems across a broad swath of parameters and with a broader mindset. This helps me today—I can design anywhere, sell anywhere, and build anywhere. That also sharpened my sensing capabilities, as I could look at things with a two-pronged lens.

While I was studying electrical engineering, I decided that I didn't want to be an electrical engineer managing power grids but wanted to bet my future on information technology. At that time, it was not possible for me to switch between engineering streams, but I figured out access to various modern technology and tools in and around my school, and I started working on software projects on the side. I wrote a few papers, including a couple that I presented to local IEEE student chapters. This helped me sense the future and got me highly motivated to get into the software industry, and I have never regretted that decision.

When I started working, I realized I wanted to be in sales and marketing, and I jumped straight in. Some of the early lessons of my work life came from there. One day, our office was open on a holiday when most customers were closed. Our sales leader gave us a simple task—identify one tall building in our area (typically ten to twelve stories high); get to the top using an elevator; and keep walking down doing cold calls to all customers who were open that day. At that time, we felt stupid and skeptical.

I started at the top of a twelve-story building, walked down the stairs checking for offices that were open. If they were open, I walked in to check if they were looking for any technology solutions. I must have done about seven in-person cold calls that day and found a couple of opportunities. That day I lost all apprehension of ever walking into a customer's office to have a discussion. Looking back, that was one of the most valuable learnings of my life. I can walk into any customer CXO's office today to have a meaningful dialogue on their business. It also creates an uncanny sensing ability, a thrill, as I walk into any customer's office, not knowing what opportunity lies therein. The colder the lead, the more excited I was, and the more challenging the opportunity was. It also helped me navigate the famous cold calling at Harvard pretty easily. I do cold calls even today, either with customers, potential recruits or community leaders and I love it.

As we look at learning from business, there are numerous examples of companies that are forced into extinction or companies that come back to life from the throes of death. Most of them were not learning fast enough or were not internalizing the learning they were getting. Companies that are able to continually sense customer needs and learn from customers to adapt and innovate continue to remain successful in business.

It will be interesting to see how traditional retailers will compete and win against the likes of Amazon. We will need to see how the future of education transforms the business model of established schools. Will traditional auto companies adapt to emerging high tech, self-driving electric cars, or will they bring more innovation in alternative fuel-based automotive? How will Internet of things (IOT) change the future of all businesses? Will traditional technology companies be successful in driving change and transformation as they address challenges from hundreds of smaller Software-as-a-service companies?

The one common trait you'll see from the examples above is that incumbents have to sustain their existing business models and trying to build new ones in parallel while being challenged by competitors who have singular focus on new business models. There is additional pressure on incumbents running two or more business models. This puts pressure on people, resources, and funding.

Some big companies are unable to manage and handle this pressure. I have seen frequent examples of start-and-stop mentality among big companies on strategic initiatives. They start something and shut it down in a couple of years to move on to something else. After a few years, they realize their mistake and come back to it, by which time, it is too late.

Big companies need to drive sustained effort on a few initiatives while driving consistency and playing for the long term. Figuring out which initiatives need to be funded for the long term requires good sensing abilities, solid data, and customer centricity.

Twelve

Customer Centricity and Monetization

We see our customers as invited guests to a party, and we are the hosts. It's our job every day to make every important aspect of the customer experience a little bit better.

—JEFF BEZOS

Monetization and customer experience is one of my favorite topics for a business discussion. Whenever I look through business plans, I always search for the customer acquisition and monetization plan. People assume that customer acquisition is easy and that once you have customers, you can monetize easily because customers will pay for your goods and services.

However, this is not how things play out in most businesses. Acquiring a customer and creating a revenue stream is one of the most difficult aspects of running a business. How do you create profitable businesses while doing the most to acquire customers and make them happy? New companies (and startups) jump in early into business, thinking that hiring a business-development person will solve the customer-acquisition problem for them.

Of late, I have been talking to a lot of IOT startups. After spending two or more years to build a product, they are desperately looking for customers. This is a tricky approach because customer requirements are changing fast and technology is changing rapidly. In our venture, we decided to flip things around by starting with customer-use cases first. Four out of five startup business plans that I have look through do not have clearly defined monetization plans.

If you look at bigger companies, they usually have established customer-acquisition teams and monetization models. Their problem (in many cases) is that their business models and monetization plans turn rusty and are not reviewed till they are challenged by a competitor, by which time it is too late to do anything. And by that time, they have done so many small tweaks to the business model that they don't know where to start or what to improve.

All organizations have to prioritize between customer acquisition and customer experience to drive profitability. A business model is an act of creating a balance between how much you spend to acquire customers and the value you deliver to them as measured against profits you would earn. One could argue that newer and modern businesses need more focus on customer acquisitions. If you don't have customers, you don't make money.

Traditional companies or companies transforming their businesses and getting into new business models find it more difficult to answer this straightforwardly. They need money to keep the wheels running, so how do they balance profitability and customer experience? It gets more challenging if they have to balance between multiple business models at the same time.

Customer acquisition is all about creating new sources of revenue generation while staying profitable. It is as much about expanding your portfolio with existing customers as it is about opening up new ones.

Customer experience is all about keeping it simple and delighting the customer through the entire life cycle of engagement. Customer experience is mostly measured today through narrow point-in-time experiences e.g., feedback from an event or feedback from a flying experience. Usually, these narrow experience measures are not correlated across a broader spectrum of customer engagement. In addition, there is a need to accurately define the life cycle of engagement in a way that it matters to a customer, maybe broader than what it is today.

Telecalling businesses are an interesting example to look at. They typically don't fall within the purview of a narrow engagement life cycle, but you would engage with them either before or after an actual event. Consider a situation where you just got off a flight for a day trip, and your flight landed late. You realize you need to change your return flight. You call the teleagent who has no insight into your previous flight being late. Added to your woes, he is not able to guarantee you a seat on the new return flight you are hoping to catch. You need to stay over for the night. You probably spent ten or fifteen minutes (after multiple menu options) trying to sort things out. You experience is now doubly soured.

The poor teleagent had no way of knowing what happened to you before you called him other than what you might have told him. In this case, the teleagent is significantly distanced from the core business to not know enough, is less empowered, and is not in a position to prioritize a solution for your predicament. In such a situation, a tele-engine might become a weak link in a customer experience life cycle. Companies invest in telemodels to reduce cost and expand reach, but are they really empowered to making them profitable?

I am using tele-engine purely as an example here and not trying to beat down the business model. Telecalling agencies and teams are good at their work, but if they are not empowered or close to the business, they cannot do much.

Continuing with this example, I polled a few people on their experience with tele-agencies. Most of them said that their problems are usually not resolved by talking to telecallers because agents are not empowered to make difficult decisions, which is why you want to talk to somebody in the first place. If tele-engines are an important part of your business, you need to empower the agents and get them closer to the business, or their value-creation capabilities are limited.

As companies build businesses, driving consistent customer experience is of utmost importance. An experience is a perception of exposure across various customer touch points in a single journey. A bunch of experiences can combine to create a larger experience. If any touch point is a weak link in a journey, it impacts the overall experience. All touch points need to measure up to a desirable standard that organizations can predefine. There are times when exceptional performance across touch points is negated by a single below-threshold performance at one of them. Sometimes that same exceptional performance carries the weight of below-average performances through the value chain.

An airline experience is a great way to calibrate this. A poor experience at check-in can be covered up by a warm pilot or crew. If they provide that extra drink or snack, that might even make things look better. Finally, if baggage arrives quickly, that's even better. The experience is an aggregation of all the micro experiences across the journey, and they all add up to the final score. You could even add a weight to some points over others.

I used the airline industry as an example because it is an easy one to follow. This is true for all industries and functions.

Experience at a bank comprises of the various functions starting from the ATM to loan disbursements. Buying groceries is determined by the quality of groceries and the time it takes for billing at the point of sale. How would you map customer experience across multiple touch points?

Identify what really matters to customers, and focus on relevant touch points in a broad experience zone. (Airline: call customers with an offer if their flight is significantly delayed and they have a return flight the same day.)

Lesser touch points are better supported by frequency and weight measured in terms of importance. (Bank: Don't have multiple checkpoints when processing a loan; keep it compliant, and keep it simple.)

Have highly empowered response teams across the engagement life cycle. (Financial services: if you have an offer, be ready to customize on the fly)

Collect data (Internet-of-things solutions) across all the touch points, and run algorithms to understand patterns. Take actions based on those insights to improve customer experience. (Energy: I would really like to know how to reduce energy consumption.)

Drive targeted offers and promotions based on above insights (Retail: Know why I am in the store, help me find what I want and give me offers for that.)

I was looking for a home loan some time ago. I spoke to a bank, and they advised me to wait for a representative to call. The representative called back and clarified most of my doubts. I asked for an application form. It was sent to me few days later. When I had more queries, a different person spoke with me. I filled in my application form; the bank had additional questions. It had already taken fifteen days, and I did not have anything concrete in my hand. I was fed up and frustrated.

I come across a second bank that asked me to meet with a representative. She patiently answered all queries, walked me through the application form and helped me to fill it out, and checked with her credit department about the sufficiency of the application. In a span of sixty minutes, she gave me all the answers I needed that the other bank could not provide in fifteen days. This saved time for me and for the bank through a reduced number of touch points and a more empowered person. This was an example of a highly activated person who delighted me with her customer skills. If you have hired the right people, empower them as much as possible, and they will hit the ball out of the park every time.

There is another parameter involved here that I would call a loading condition. A loading condition primarily defines the preconditions to a customer experience. Did my discussion at home in the morning impact the rest of the work day? Did the last meeting at the office continue to stay on my mind and impact dinner with the family? A good-news or positive situation always elates you for a period of time, and that is a loading condition for the rest of the day. Similarly, bad news also impacts the rest of the day in a negative way. That, too, is a loading condition. Loading condition is an important consideration because it impacts your customer-experience life cycle.

A couple of airlines send limos to pick up and drop off business-class customers for their flights. That is not part of the usual experience of a passenger, but it influences experience before and after the life cycle starts. They are managing a loading condition. You can determine customer loading conditions and use those levers effectively to dial up or dial down customer engagement. Imagine giving a free app to consumers after they bought phones and left your store. Or imagine empowered employees giving away gifts or discounts at select times of the day—totally determined by how they decide to do it.

Companies have to master the art of running multiple business models together. This will have inherent complexities and challenges of management but will also be a highly customer-centric model designed to drive high profitability. As you work on multiple business models, it is usually difficult to stretch your existing teams to take on new transformational tasks that are not logical extensions of what they are already doing. You need to invest in new teams and help them prioritize customer-acquisition and experience goals. It is almost like running parallel teams to focus on existing businesses while creating new ones. How do you keep these teams engaged and activated at the same time? How do you map your people so that they are working on the right opportunities?

At this stage, I would like to introduce a term called "return on customer engagement" (ROCE). ROCE refers to the returns that you get from a customer against the investments that you make across all touch points. Just like the business model, each organization defines it their own way to meet their business goals. This will primarily depend on the level of customization and mapping investments versus outcomes for a specific customer.

We should look at profitability as determined by return on customer engagement. If we are looking at a situation of differentiated business models, you need to measure monetization and profitability for each customer over a predefined time frame. The customer-engagement process is far more granular today than it ever was, given the amount of data we now capture on everything.

Looking at profitability across each customer provides us with an accurate picture of how much money we are making and the levers we could use to tweak each customer engagement and experience. For example, if we are making less money with a large customer, we could either sense more opportunities or reduce some of the investments into that customer and deploy them elsewhere.

In general, a business is probably losing more money with a lot of customers and making more with a few. Given that we live in the world of data, it is possible to manage and monitor customer engagement on a micro level to determine investments and profitability by customer type. It is time we start looking at profitability by customer over a defined lifecycle. Whether engaging with businesses or with consumers, it is time to start thinking of return on each customer engagement. This will help you make disproportionate but aligned investments in customer acquisitions, measure the cost and impact of a consistent customer experience, and integrate various functions within the organization to function in harmony toward a common objective.

What drives profitability? Customers would pay for solutions that create aspirational advantage for them or meet a need or solve a problem. If I make a generalized statement, most companies have fixed-pricing and monetization models that hinge largely around cost, usage, and discounting.

In the new world, business-to-business monetization models have to be customized to each customer—inherently structured differently and based on what drives profitability through each customer. These monetization models are designed to be optimal for the customer while creating the highest profitability for the company. This will be like customizing business models for individual customers through customer-centric plans and measuring through "return on customer engagement"

First, you need to understand the costs involved. At a high level, the total cost will equate to the cost involved in servicing a customer, end to end. We'll use traditional business methods coupled with new data analytical models to derive this. There are several ways to go about this. We need to first identify measurable touch points. We then assign weights to each touch point. Finally, we calculate the cost of touch points for each customer.

Once you have identified the cost, you need to determine profitability by subtracting the cost from the monetization received from the customer. Your total profits will be an aggregation of profits across all touch points and customers. This is a simplified view of measuring profitability but a more granular, data-driven way to do it.

Your marketing approach also needs to change along with the customer-engagement approach. How do you brand and position to a narrower set of customers? Each individual customer could even have a unique business model. We need to evolve micro-branding and micropositioning strategies that narrowly map to a customer need. Extensive use of data-based modern tools and techniques for this purpose.

You have probably read about the missionary or mercenary approach to business. A mercenary company wakes up every morning trying to figure out how to win against competition, make money, and thereby win customers. A missionary company wakes up trying to enlighten and inspire customers and create relationships, which enables customers to work with them.

There is a third category that I introduced earlier called "sensetionary" (connected with the ability to sense), which is an alternate model to driving customer engagement. In the "sensetionary" model, companies determine the right approach to business based on individual customers.

Some business models and customers might require a combination of missionary and mercenary tactics or one or the other at a specific point of time. The reality is that in the new world, each model might not exist in isolation, and it will all depend on the opportunity being sensed and worked on.

Thirteen

The SCORE Framework

Everyone here has the sense that right now is

one of those moments when we are influencing

the future.

—STEVE JOBS

C reating aspirational advantage for a customer is the ultimate engagement model to drive superior experience for
the customer and higher profitability for your business. We have
covered various "big company" themes in this book, and I wanted
to conclude with a framework that can help you implement some
of these ideas and practices in your business. The framework
is called SCORE. The more you implement, the more you can

score for your organization, and the better aspirational advantage you can deliver for your customers.

S = Sense

C = Culture

O = Organize

R = Risk

E = Engage

SENSE

Sensing is the key to success and will help you stay ahead of the curve to provide aspirational advantage to customers. It can help you respond proactively to customer requirements and address aspirations rather than just solve problems.

When I was a seller in the IT industry, I rarely lost a critical deal because I trained myself to sense all the time. Sensing strengthens your understanding of the market landscape, the environment, and the ecosystem around your business. You cannot take a software developer and expect that person to sense opportunities in the retail industry—unless (maybe), we are talking about online retail. There has to be context to the whole thing.

The human brain processes what you sense by matching it with patterns in the environment, ecosystem, and landscape that exist in our minds. There are no playbooks here, and this is not rocket science—sense the market, sense what customers are looking for, pitch what you are passionate about, and find out the customer's aspiration. Use data to validate what you sense so that it is more than just gut feel, and you are able to defend it. Staying connected with your customers is important and will help you understand their aspirations and where they are headed. I always try to map to an aspiration and not to a problem—because the answer to an aspiration is what will create more value for the customer.

CULTURE

Culture is the single most important attribute that makes or breaks organizations. If culture and change does not flow through the organization, it will eventually go downhill. If the culture valve is turned in the right direction, they can drive significant change and positivity in the organization. If leaders can collectively turn the culture valve the same amount and in the right direction, they can create a cultural revolution in their organization.

Culture is also the most extensible and infectious thing on the planet. It spreads rapidly and engulfs people without leaving immediate signs of how or what happened. So, leaders need to be authentic when talking about culture.

Several years ago, I came across a leader who was passionate about culture. He had a lot of ideas and made broad communications about how he wanted to change culture. Over a period of time, it became hard to implement because there were inconsistencies in his approach and people stared to lose faith. In addition, he had filled his leadership team with faithful people who would broadly agree to his point of view, thereby closing out all options of constructive feedback. Eventually, he was not able to rally people around him and had to quit.

It is important for organizations to reward people for demonstrating culture attributes and being culture champions in the organization. I always look for people who would believe in the culture and would be great evangelists of it in the organization or the group. Culture is a combination of strategy and practice, and both have to happen.

ORGANIZE (AND MODERNIZE)

Doing business in the new world using old-school techniques will not work irrespective of the industry you are in. The pace of change might be different in different industries, but you still need to adapt to change and the new ways of the business world. Whether it is the way you use data, motivate your employees, or drive customer engagement, you need to organize and modernize.

Consider an example of consulting firms. Will customers continue to invest millions of dollars trying to get specialized consulting services? Or will consulting practices modernize enough that everything will be available online with advanced machine-learning capabilities that can determine and customize consulting solutions for clients? What if a machine-learning algorithm could sift through millions of records on a manufacturing problem and come up with suggestions on a couple of solutions that might just work for another manufacturing company? This would probably take a few hours, compared to months of hard work that several consultants and research analysts would need to put in. It may not end up replacing analysts and consultants, it will change their job significantly, reduce time to market for customers (and save cost), and provide solutions that have worked elsewhere.

Education is another industry that is undergoing significant transformation. Consider business education for example. One part of education that corresponds to content-based learning can be easily delivered through online tools and modern learning processes. Another part of education is about practice and networking that might still need in-person interactions. The advent of online learning is just the tip of the iceberg. You need both models to be successful. And things might be different in different parts of the world.

In addition to changes in learning models, the fundamentals of what we learn and why we learn will change. We could have robots running classrooms and working as teaching assistants. There will be some aspects of online learning and in-person learning that will merge to create hybrid models. One such example is the MOOC (massive open online course) that uses best practices from both worlds to deliver training.

It is the era of marketing and data-driven business models—there is transformation in marketing, enabled by data and new tools. The key discussion is servicing the customer through various customized touch points to deliver ultimate customer experience across the customer life cycle.

Different people use different tools at work or play. SMS/text messaging is virtually dead and is vanishing from the modern world. Use of social media, modern technology, automation, and modern practices is a must—the more you delay, the more you have to catch up. I cannot emphasize enough the need to get a solid acquaintance with data. Data will be the king and will be a key attribute for a business to survive in the new world.

RISK

Risk taking is an important attribute for success. Create an environment for people to feel empowered to take risks. Promote strong people practices that encourage and reward a risk-taking culture in an organization. Keep adapting and reinvesting into your business model and look at your business model on an ongoing basis before the alarm bells ring. When you peak with great profitability, good revenue, strong market share, and a solid pipeline, this would be a good time to review your business model.

When you hear about a competitor multiple times (especially from customers), take notice. You know how hard it is for a startup or for a new entrant to get to a customer. If the customer knows about it and talks about it, you should take notice.

Finally, make sure that the boundaries of risk taking are appropriately defined, especially as you work across different countries across the world. Risk taking has to be ethical, compliant, and responsible.

ENGAGE

Move away from problem solving, orchestration, and inward-facing approaches to helping customers get aspirational advantage and helping them invest for the future.

More and more customers today are looking for forward-looking solutions—it is not enough to solve a current problem. How do you find business-model innovation that can help customers innovate for the future? Customers are looking for more customized engagement models that, in turn, will get us to look at each individual customer's profitability—a win-win situation for both.

Be thoroughly updated about your products and services. Customers are more informed today than ever before, and they always know more about their environments. This combination will make your customers more knowledgeable than you. Everybody in the organization is a buyer now—the specialization is gone, and you need to target a broad swath of people. The line between various profiles of decision makers is blurred. You need to be at the helm of innovation all the time. Innovation does not reside only within engineering or the factory anymore; it is also about reverse engineering that starts with the customer and works backward. Firefighting days are gone; separate the firefighters from innovators. It is really about innovation and forward sensing.

In this era when things are changing fast, product life cycles are getting cut. You do not have time to set strategy and execute one at a time. You will need to innovate and work on multiple strategies and business models at the same time.

Every customer is a partner, vendor, and supplier somewhere, and the entropy of global business stays the same. Shifts in any industry, ecosystem, or business model likely impact others. Extend your business model to vendors, suppliers, and partners. These extensions and connected work flows will drive superior experience across a customer life cycle. Get the crowd on your side early on, and learn from the crowd—if people don't like or use something, chances that they will use it later are remote.

In the new world, even big companies need to behave like smaller companies. People need to be hands-on and agile to respond to customer opportunities faster. Have solid practices in place to hire and retain the best talent for your company. Create a highly empowered and risk-taking culture that can sense and innovate faster than anybody else.

Author Biography

The CEO of Seattle-based technology venture IOT World Labs, Jaideep Sen has over twenty-two years of experience working with such presti-gious companies as Microsoft, Intel, and Compaq/HP.

Sen holds an engineering degree from NIT Durgapur, an MBA from Jadavpur University, and PLD from Harvard Business School. He has lived and worked across the globe, primarily in North America and Asia.

An avid reader of business and fiction books, Sen contributes to social causes focused on education and children's health.

www.ingramcontent.com/pod-product-compliance
Lightning Source LLC
Chambersburg PA
CBHW070241190526
45169CB00001B/251